MW00532571

"Carol Weis's *Stumbling Home* is a story of recovery, a reckoning of the relationships that complicate it, and an examination of the years that brought her to that last flute of champagne. A welcome addition to the addiction canon, Weis's vivid narrative illuminates the experience of navigating alcoholism and recovery as a woman with clarity and piercing details."　　　　　　　　—Erin Khar, author of *Strung Out*

"Frank, searing, and ultimately hopeful, *Stumbling Home* is a page-turning story of alcoholism, relationships, and hard-won healing. Any reader whose life has been impacted by addiction will see themselves in these pages. I certainly did."
　　　　　—Kristi Coulter, author of *Nothing Good Can Come from This*

"Bravely confronting the fears and the feelings that go along with addiction, recovery, and just being human, *Stumbling Home* will resonate with so many of us. Carol Weis inspires while reminding us that we are never alone."
　　　　　　　—Lisa F. Smith, author of *Girl Walks Out of a Bar*

"Raw and naked, Carol Weis's *Stumbling Home* makes clear the connection between childhood trauma and substance use, plus adult dysfunction."
　　　　　　　　　　　—Ann Dowsett Johnston,
　　　author of *Drink: The Intimate Relationship Between Women and Alcohol*

"In frank, lyrical prose and a nonlinear structure, Weis draws seemingly paradoxic parallels between her own alcoholism and recovery, single motherhood, and childhood trauma. In so doing, she demonstrates the myriad ways in which the expectations put upon women and girls shape our shared experiences and cultural conceptions of femininity and what it means to exist in a woman's body."
　　　　　　　　　—Amy Long, author of *Codependence*

"From the riveting opening to the reconciliation of the end, *Stumbling Home* links the anxiety of abandonment to the anxiety of addiction with exceptional clarity and resonance. In exploring both her family and her own personal history with alcohol, Weis offers a memoir punctuated by reckoning, empathy for who we were against who we can become, and layers of grace and vulnerability."
　　　　　　　　　　　—Wendy J. Fox,
　　　author of *If the Ice Had Held* and *What If We Were Somewhere Else*

Stumbling Home

Life Before and After That Last Drink

CAROL WEIS

Heliotrope Books
New York

"16 Steps for Discovery and Empowerment" by Charlotte Davis Kasl, Ph.D., is excerpted on page231 from *Many Roads, One Journey: Moving Beyond the 12 Steps* © Charlotte Kasl. Originally published by HarperCollins and reprinted with permission from Dr. Kasl and HarperCollins.

Cover by Carol Weis with Heliotrope Books
Designed and Typeset by Heliotrope Books

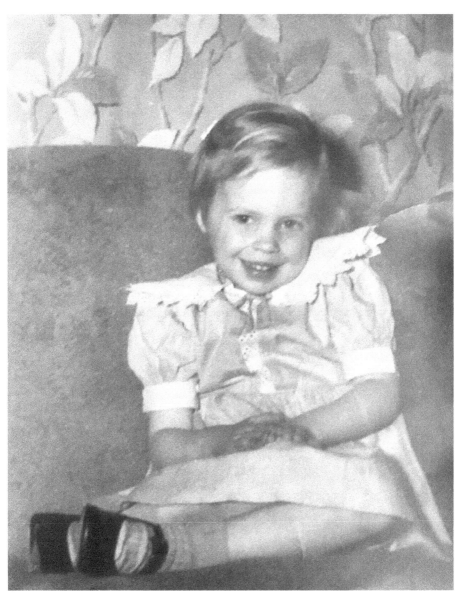

Three-year-old me

Also by Carol Weis:

When the Cows Got Loose
Divorce Papers

Table of Contents

Prologue

What happens to a child who's abandoned
           intentionally or not
                 when she grows up?
A girl whose early years are rife
with anger and fear
who confuses trouble with fun
and who's terrified of being left again?

She ends up drinking and drugging
way more than she should
seeking to obliterate her past
sleeping with every Tim, Rich, and Henry
with her claws ever extended
eventually marrying a guy she snags
who consumes as much as she does
fathers her child
and fulfilling her fears
leaves her when she gets sober
unable to do so himself.

This woman-child stumbles and falls
over and over again
           until finally
      she picks herself up
and stumbles home.

For Maggie,
who came to me
to help me get sober.

Foreword

I've spent much of my life caught in a web of anxiety, trapped in a tangle of fears. Constantly worried that I wasn't smart enough, cool enough, or capable enough. I swore I'd never find someone to love me, or worse, when I did, I'd scare them away. I felt inadequate and unlovable. Bottom line: I just wasn't good enough.

Being an adult frightened the hell out of me.

So, as many young people do, I turned to alcohol.

We live in an age where fear and anxiety are heightened by things like the climate crisis, gun violence, and acts of terrorism, both foreign and domestic. These kinds of fears often make people drink more than they should. The 24/7 cable news cycle, along with the vast array of social media sites and news apps, all contribute to a condition called *Headline Stress Disorder** that apparently affects women more than men. It may be a reason why women's alcohol use has risen so dramatically (84% in a 10 year period**). If you stay up later to watch the news and pour yourself an extra glass of wine, or order another bottle from one of the alcohol delivery services, or you're a member of a Facebook group like *Moms Who Need Wine*, you might see a bit of yourself in me.

One of my biggest fears came from a much deeper place than what's on the news. Things that happened in my childhood caused a relentless fear of abandonment, which colored all my relationships, especially with men. At first, drinking squelched the fear, and it was fun. Until it eventually lost its fun factor and became something I thought about constantly, something I had to do. After a while, I found I needed to increase my alcohol intake to get the same numbing effect. It took a long time for me to accept I had a problem.

I've been sober for 31 years. I miraculously stayed sober through the trials of single parenting. Through 9/11, through Sandy Hook and other mass shootings, and through all the bedlam surrounding Trump's presidency and the coronavirus pandemic, breathing deeply to fend off the fear.

*A term coined by couples therapist, Steven Stosny, Ph.D.

**From a JAMA Psychiatry Study on Alcohol Use Disorders

So if you or someone you love may be drinking more than usual to relieve the stress and fear the news cycle produces or to push down painful feelings and issues from the past, perhaps my story will help.

That is my hope.

With much love,
Carol

Author's Note

The events in this book are based on my own memories and taken from various conversations with others. Some people may have different recollections from what I've depicted, which often happens. I've also changed the names of a few individuals.

One, two, three, one, two, three, drink.
Throw 'em back till I lose count.
~ from *Chandelier* by Sia

chapter one

The End

The last drink I have is a flute of champagne.

It's New Year's Eve.

My husband reserves a special room for us at a nearby hotel. He buys an imperial bottle of Moët, a misplaced purchase for this particular occasion. We're making a last-ditch effort at saving our marriage. A gala erupts in the ballroom below, where we journey to join the revelers.

Lights twinkle, streamers hang, and chandeliers glisten.

I hardly notice.

The band plays songs that were once my favorites.

I hardly hear.

Hoards of gleeful couples celebrate around us.

We dance with them, pretending to have a good time.

But I know the end is creeping near.

My husband's been having an affair with a woman half his age. He hasn't come clean yet, but my gut knows something's going on. So I bleach my hair a sassier shade of blond, starve myself in hopes of losing the weight I know he hates, and turn myself inside out to get him to notice me again.

But mostly I drink.

Because of my Catholic upbringing, I have a list of rules I follow.

My commandments of drinking. I only have three. Ten is too many.

1) No drinking before 5:00. I watch the clock tick away the minutes. It drives me crazy.

2) No drinking on Tuesdays or Thursdays. I break this all the time. It's impossible not to.

3) No hard liquor. Only wine and beer. I feel safe drinking those.

Anything else means, well, I've become my parents.

Or even worse, his. I can't bear to go there.

One night, when he takes off for a weekend conference, or so he says, I get so stinking drunk after tucking my daughter in for the night, I puke all over our pinewood floor. All over those rich amber boards I spent hours resurfacing with him, splattering my guts out next to our once sexually active and gleaming brass bed.

Tarnished now from months of disuse.

The following morning, my five-year-old daughter, with sleep encircling her concerned eyes, stands there staring at me, her bare feet immersed in clumps of yellow. The scrambled eggs I managed to whip up the night before are scattered across our bedroom floor, reeking so bad, I'm certain I'll start retching again. I look down at the mess I made with little recollection of how it got there, then peer at my daughter, her eyes oozing the compassion of an old soul as she says, "Oh Mommy. Are you sick?"

Shame grips every part of my trembling body. Its menacing hands, a vice around my pounding head. I can't bear to look in her eyes. The fear of not remembering how I've gotten here is palpable. Every morsel of its terror is strewn across my barf-laden tongue and I'm certain my daughter knows the secret I've kept from myself and others for years.

You're an alcoholic. You can't hide it anymore.

Every last thread of that warm cloak of denial gets ripped away, and here I am, gazing into the eyes of my five-year-old daughter who's come to yank me out of my misery.

It takes two more months for me to quit.

Two months of dragging my body, heavy with remorse, out of that tarnished brass bed to send my daughter off to school. Then crawling back into it and staying there, succumbing to the disjointed sleep of depression. Until the bus drops her off hours later, as her little finger, filled with endless kindergarten stories, pokes me awake.

Each poke like being smacked in the face with my failures as a mother.

And then New Year's Eve shows up and I dress in a slinky black outfit, a color fitting my descending mood, a dress I buy to win him back. The husband who, 12 years before, drives hundreds of miles to pursue this wayward woman, wooing me over a dinner I painstakingly prepare, as I allow myself to wonder if he in fact, may be *the one*. We dine on the roof of the 3rd floor apartment I rent on 23rd and Walnut, in the heart of Philadelphia where I work as a chef, and where I tell him over a bottle of crisp chardonnay that I might be an alcoholic. He laughs and convinces me I'm not. He knows what alcoholics look like. Growing up with two of them, he assures me I am nothing like his parents.

His mother, a sensuous woman with flaming hair and lips to match, passes out in the car on late afternoons after spending hours carousing with her best friend, a woman he's grown to despise. Coming home from school, day after day, he finds her slumped on the bench seat of their black Buick sedan, dragging her into the house to make dinner for him and his little brother and sister, watching as she staggers around their kitchen. His father, a noted attorney in his early years, drinks until he can't see and rarely comes home for supper. He loses his prestigious position in the law firm he fought to get into, and gets half his jaw removed from the mouth cancer he contracts from his unrestrained drinking. He dies at 53, a lonely and miserable man.

"I know what alcoholics look like," he says. "You're not one of them."

I grab onto his reassurance and hold it tight.

And with that we polish off the second bottle of chardonnay, crawl back through the kitchen window and slither onto the black-and-white checkered tile floor, in a haze of lust and booze, before we creep our way into my tousled and beckoning bed. It takes me another twelve years to hit bottom, to peek into the eyes of the only child I bring into this world, reflecting the shame I've carted around most of my life.

So on New Year's Eve, we make our way up in the hotel elevator. After crooning Auld Lang Syne with the crowd of other booze-laden partiers still hanging on to the evening's festivities, as the bitter taste of letting go of something so dear, so close to my heart, seeps into my psyche. A woman who totters next to me still sings the song, with red stilettos dangling from her fingers. Her drunken haze reflects in my eyes as she nearly slides down the elevator wall.

At that moment, I see myself.

The realization reluctantly stumbles down the hall with me, knowing that gleaming bottle of Moët waits with open arms in the silver bucket we crammed with ice before leaving the room. Ripping off the foil encasing the lip of the bottle, my husband quickly unfastens the wire cage and pops the cork that hits the ceiling of our fancy room. Surely an omen for what follows. He carefully pours the sparkling wine, usually a favorite of mine, into two leaded flutes huddling atop our nightstand, making sure to divide this liquid gold evenly into the tall, slim goblets that leave rings at night's end. We lift our glasses and make a toast, to the New Year and to us, though our eyes quickly break the connection, telling a different story.

As soon as the bubbles hit my lips, from the wine that always evokes such tangible joy and plasters my tongue with memories, I know the gig's up. It tastes like poison. I force myself to drink more, a distinctly foreign concept, coercing a smile that squirms across my face. I nearly gag as I continue to shove the bubbly liquid down my throat, not wanting to hurt my husband's feelings, who spent half a week's pay on this desperate celebration. But with each sip I take, my brain and body scream *you freaking alcoholic,* and I know at that moment I can no longer do this. When I put down that glass, on this fateful New Year's Eve, I know I'll never bring another ounce of liquor to my lips.

I'm done.

There's no turning back.

And as we tuck ourselves into bed, I keep it to myself.

Each kiss that night is loaded with self-loathing and disgust.

Those twelve years of knowing squeezes tightly into a fist of shame.

Little does my husband know, if he climbs on top of me,

he'll be making love to death itself.

Instead, I turn the other way and cry myself silently to sleep.

Your days of drinking have finally come to an end.

And you can't help but wonder…

will your marriage follow?

chapter two

The Beginning

I have my first drink in the cellar of my childhood home. I'm 16. And more than ready to investigate the intoxicating allure of my parents' favorite pastime. My friend, Karey, whose boobs are twice the size of mine and who frequently declares with great enthusiasm, we-must-we-must-we-must-increase-our-bust, while grasping hands to forearms and pumping away, is my accomplice in this particular crime. She jiggles beside me behind my father's prized possession: the built-in bar that huddles in the corner at the foot of our cellar stairs. The bar that Mom declared was a crucial selling point when she and Dad bought the house.

Most importantly, it's stocked to the hilt with every alcoholic beverage these inquiring teens can imagine. Bottles of Canadian Club and Seagram's, Tanqueray and Smirnoff, Johnny Walker Red and Jim Beam, Meyer's Rum, Tawny Port, Dry Sack Sherry, and one of Mom's favorite, Leroux Peppermint Schnapps. They all stand at attention, yearning to be poured into those precious little shot glasses that balance on their rims along the edge of the bar. Unable to decide which one to taste, we proceed to try them all.

All in the same tumbler.

Resulting in a throat-blazing, dizzy-producing

gag-worthy, don't-ever-do-this-again kind of venture.

"Oh god, this is disgusting!"

And yes, it's a disastrous experiment.

Except for one thing.

One game-changing thing.

That thing that ignites my senses and won't let go.

The thing they call the bu-z-z-z-z-z.

That ever-loving, blurry-making, loopty-looing buzz. Sent straight from the neurotransmitter gods, rushing to my brain. Filled with the promise my upbringing can't deliver. Instant relief from the anxiety and fear that ceaselessly stalks me, like a swarm of killer bees, ready to strike.

I sense from that day forward, I'm hooked.

Not with the taste.

But with the buzz.

As I hold my nose and finish off the last of our vomitous concoction.

This was bound to happen, as I come from a family of drinkers. Mostly on my mom's side, as Dad hailed from a clan of Christian Science teetotalers from which he quickly strayed. On her father's side, Mom was both Irish and Catholic. A seemingly hazardous combination when it comes to alcohol use.

My granddad grew up on a modest plantation, with three brothers and two sisters, in the southern town of Vidalia, Louisiana, not long after the Reconstruction years were over. He was a sweet man, with a large sweet tooth to match, and often chased down the ice cream truck on a hot summer day. He had no qualms about using the n-word, which I'm still healing from, and sense was part of the everyday slang that was tossed around his Louisiana home.

He also drank.

Though my parents were daily drinkers, Grandpa was a binger. His worst days followed my grandma's death, the woman my mom called *Mother*—who preferred Mom's older sister, Lucia, over her—a bias Mom repeated with my sister and me. Grandma hardly drank at all and died of bladder cancer when I was in sixth grade. Her funeral produced a bad case of giggles between my cousin, Merry, and me, as they lowered her shiny casket into the ground.

Grandpa split those years living six months at our house and six months at Aunt Lu's. He'd get all gussied up, put on his straw boater, climb into his old green DeSoto with its brown leather seats—the car I took on a few spins before I had my license—and off he'd go to who knows where. That is until hours later when he'd careen into the driveway, barely missing the trash cans that stood guard, waiting for his return.

Mom eventually confiscated his keys, which didn't stop Grandpa. Determined to squelch the demons, he'd climb the steep hill where our West Orange house sat admiring the New York skyline, to catch the DeCamp bus that rumbled down Northfield Avenue, carting him to the surplus of pubs scattered about a mile or so from our home. More than once, he'd return via police cruiser, occasionally with a bruise somewhere on his increasingly fragile frame. He'd do this for a few weeks, dispel the demons from his system, and then he'd stop.

Until they rose in revolt.

And off he'd go again.

My sister, Sui, recalled the agony of seeing him literally clinging to a lamppost, barely able to stand on his own, then climbing aboard the same DeCamp bus she took home from high school. Slumping in the seat, hoping he wouldn't see her, she cringed at every boisterous remark that escaped his mouth. To top it off, she'd have to escort him down that same steep hill, holding him steady so he wouldn't topple over.

Grandpa held the alcohol gene in our family.

And it spread around our tribe like quenchless fire.

Mom stood, along with her sister, Lucia, directly in the flames until she was 86-years-old. Sadly, we were forced to put her in a nursing home after she took a death-defying fall that battered and bruised half of her already frail torso. None of us could believe her poor body withstood all the liquor she poured into it for all those years.

My mother was a beautiful woman whose laughter spread quickly around a room. She radiated warmth and had a joyful spirit, and was trapped in her generation's expectations of the role of women. Her big regrets were never going to college and not getting her teeth fixed.

And marrying my dad.

She once told me she married him because all the other men she cared for had died in the war. Dad pursued her until she relented and said yes. Apparently on their wedding day, she lay prostrate across a bed, while her sister massaged her back, trying to release the knots in her taut muscles.

Only two months into the marriage, she felt she'd made a mistake.

But she stuck it out and had the babies she always wanted. My sister and I came first, with a stillborn in between. Just after my first younger brother was born, when I wasn't quite three years old, Mom contracted tuberculosis. Something she attributed to the pleurisy she developed after riding in a convertible with the top down, garbed in a wet bathing suit from a day at the beach. During her infirmary, we were scattered about, staying with various relatives and family friends while she grieved in a sanatorium for eighteen long months.

I was shipped off within three weeks of my first placement from all the wailing I did, curled up on my cousin's bed, a ball of toddler grief. And then after six months or so with the second family, where an unfortunate accident occurred, I was sent off again to another location. My third (and last) placement would be my undoing.

Something that chased me for 35 years.

Something I wouldn't come to grips with until after I got sober.

As we struggled in different ways from her absence, my mom also suffered. Her longing and guilt ate away at her, leaving three children for this span of time felt interminable. And back in those days, feelings like that were rarely processed verbally, certainly not in a constructive way. Upon her release from the hospital, those tangle of emotions were washed down with Old Fashioned cocktails and glasses of port. And in time, the sherry she poured from a brown bag while preparing dinner.

Eventually, one or two drinks were never enough.

When I was six, Mom relapsed and was hospitalized again, for nearly a year. My second brother was born six months prior, and the burden of that birth while caring for three other young children was too much for her body to bear. This time we stayed at home, with Dad's sister coming in to care for us, unaware I'm sure of what she was getting herself into.

My dad, who taught me to love nature, to ride a bike, and to speak my mind to men, was a handsome, Clark-Gable-ish looking man, the youngest of five kids, and ill equipped to take on a task like this. As the baby of the family, he knew little of care-giving, a job in those days the sole custody of women.

My aunt was unmarried and childless, and back then, harshly referred to as an old maid. She was as clueless as Dad. In that year of chaos, my dad rarely came home for dinner. He'd emerge half-cocked after baths were taken and we were all ready for bed. How my aunt survived that year, with four boundary-less kids turning the house upside down, is still beyond me.

We all experienced this challenge in different ways. My sister took on the role of little mother, while I slowly emerged as the female delinquent of the family. The other being my youngest brother, who in later life would spend time in jail.

I remember getting my neighborhood friend, Larry, who would one day produce the PBS favorite, *Reading Rainbow*, into pulling up the newly planted annuals in his neighbor's garden with me. I needed relief from the chaos that wrought havoc with my young abandoned self, which would one day be pushed down with the same elixir my parents enjoyed, the safe haven and reprieve that each sip of alcohol provides. Until then, things like yanking up plants would have to do.

Like many heavy drinkers, my parents fought daily. And year after year, their fighting grew more vindictive. Dad was *Who's Afraid of Virginia Wolf*'s George to Mom's Martha. One night, in a fit of rage after taunting and badgering from Mom, Dad uncharacteristically smacked her across the face, breaking her nose, along with our faith in him. My parents were not physical with their fighting; they used words to wound each other. This corporal act caused their already deteriorating marriage, from years of alcohol abuse and its fallout, to crumble even more.

My sister and I begged them to seek counsel, begged them to stop fighting, begged them to get a divorce. But most of all, we begged them to stop drinking, the cause of their marital woes, which neither of them could do.

My sister, three years my senior, left home after she graduated from college. She'd gotten a full scholarship from the US Navy in exchange for two years of active duty as a nurse. She spent those years at the Bethesda Naval Hospital caring for vets returning from Vietnam. I yearned to go away to school, prayed I'd get accepted to one of those far-off colleges where I applied. Sadly, fate had me stuck at home for another four years, acting as a conduit for my parents' arguments, four of the most depressing years of my life.

My parents stayed together in their shattered existence for 41 years, my dad continuing to work as president of his gear manufacturing company until he retired two years before his death.

He died of heart failure.

Or possibly a broken heart.

Years of living with a woman who didn't really love him, plus daily lunches of scotch-on-the-rocks, and more when he got home, finally did him in. Though the fighting with my mom was the lighter fluid to his demise.

All of this left its imprint on my psyche,

thrusting me into a life of

anxiety, codependency, and addiction.

chapter three

Amazing Grace, But Then

T he day after I stop drinking I feel relief. The knots I've carried around like rocks in my shoulders are gone. There's no shaking or trembling like many in detox do. The desire to drink has been lifted.

A major miracle has occurred.

You think of it as amazing grace.

You turn on Judy Collins and have her sing it to you.

My husband and I have appointments to see a new therapist. After begging for months to do marriage counseling, the first therapist we see is late for the appointment, rambling on about her disastrous trip to the grocery store, after making her delayed and dramatic entrance.

I'm unnerved by this behavior and never return.

This new therapist comes with a stamp of approval from the nurse practitioner at my OB/GYN, and though my hopes are high, she requests to see us separately, which fills me with dread. I'm defined by my husband's professional persona and know little of who I am beyond mother, housewife, and baker, the business I started last year, a creative outlet I'm good at and love to do.

How will you ever fill the time

with someone you've never met before?

You sound like the mother you fail to respect.

When I see this therapist, I can't stop talking. She sits in her rocking chair, scribbling notes as I speak, hanging onto every word I say. I tell her of our troubled marriage, my suspicions of my husband's affair, and my long-over-due split with my best-bud, booze. Of course, I mention my husband's drink-ing problem, too—the one he's not ready to embrace. I talk excessively of him and the problems he's caused in our marriage. She gently encourages me to attend an Al-Anon meeting.

Though I'm not quite sure what I'm doing there, I end up at one that Fri-day. I tell the folks who greet me at the door that I'm new and quit drinking on New Year's and they smile, saying I'm at the wrong meeting. They direct me to the AA room down the hall. Doing as they say, I listen quietly to the people who speak, calling themselves alcoholics. They share their stories of misery and shame, and I know instantly I'm home.

I climb aboard the pink cloud hovering over my head and take it for a ride.

I tell my husband about the kind people I met.

"You know, we're as sick as our secrets. And I only need to stay sober today," I say. As elated as I am about being abstemious, the idea of a lifetime still seems menacing.

My husband's eyes glaze over, even though he says, "Wow, that's great. I'm really happy for you." Behind that half-smile lies a trench he's hiding in, wait-ing for bombs to explode around him. His drinking is more near and dear to him than I can possibly imagine. He holds it close, like a hand in high stakes poker.

I won't know how dear until I lay my cards on the table.

My husband has his session with the new therapist. When he arrives back home, I'm in the shower. He comes into the bathroom and says he needs to tell me something.

"Can't it wait?" I say, rubbing shampoo into my hair.

"No. Renée says I need to come clean right away."

I push suds away from my eyes and wait for him to speak again, massaging my scalp deeply with my fingertips.

"I've been seeing someone else."

The shower runs hot, but I can't stop shivering. My churning brain drowns out the sound of the water. I pray I haven't heard what he said, although I know I have. It just confirms what I've already sensed. My body shakes, trembling to its core, as I let the shampoo drip into my eyes.

The sting it produces feels better than the sting of betrayal.

I long to scream, but my throat tightens up. Like a python has come up through the drain and slithered its way around my neck. My husband is still standing beyond the sliding glass doors and I don't want him to see me like this. I know lack of sex has spurred him to do this.

On second thought, maybe that's what I need to do.

Throw my naked body at him.

The confusion fills your eyes
until you break down and sob.

chapter four

Liquid Courage

Although I was a painfully shy kid who sucked my thumb into third grade and often hid in corners at family gatherings, I erupted from that web of coyness in my junior year of high school, the year I had my first drink. I became friends with a group of kids who had no qualms about hopping in a car, bathing suits beneath clothes, and scoping out wealthy neighborhoods where lavish built-in pools could be found. One night after climbing a fence and sneaking into someone's back yard, we were stunned to see a double-barrel shotgun staring us in the face. With the owner yelling at us in his skivvies.

Another night, after spending the day swimming with our guy friends at a nearby pond, my friend, Dotty, and I agreed to stash our excruciatingly sunburned bodies in the trunk of Ronnie Quarnaccio's old-codger-of-a-car to get in the drive-in free.

These things were often done with the help of some liquid courage.

By senior year, my popularity had taken off. Giving the guys free-reign of the pool table hunkered in the basement of our house helped the cause. They'd often knock on the door asking, "Mind if we play some pool?" My parents, who remained mostly under the influence through our teen years, were always happy to see me staying home rather than traipsing around town in someone else's car.

This group of guys seemed to be my friends, until a note delivered to my front door stating, "Suck my dick, you horny slut" read quite differently, and phone calls repeating the same demeaning words polluted me with connotations I didn't understand. As far as I knew, I was still a virgin, as heavy petting was the furthest I'd let myself go.

As a good Catholic girl, I was forbidden anything more.

That same year, our football team was undefeated and mid-season it was decided we'd hold a party at my parents' summer cottage on Culver's Lake. The same house where my youngest brother at 12, brewed his own beer in the confines of his tiny, ceiling-less room.

We met at the school parking lot and piled into cars that carried us north to Sussex County, where our lake house sat quietly awaiting. When we pulled into the driveway and various spots on the lawn, I panicked when trunks popped open, fully loaded with cases of Pabst Blue Ribbon, way more than the 50 or so teens that made the hour-long drive could possibly drink. Even so, I was oddly grateful they hadn't confiscated the giant Pabst beer bottle that hovered over the Newark skyline.

When the cops arrived, a mere hour into the debauchery, after a number of boys pulled a *Stand By Me* stunt, bashing mailboxes with baseball bats long before the movie was made, I knew I was in deep doo-doo. We were blasted out of our gourds, standing ankle-deep in beer that plastered the tile floor. While being interrogated by one of the officers, my friend Dotty exclaimed, "I amn't intoxicated," which became our drunk tagline following this notorious bash.

I was grounded for the rest of our football season. It was a bitter pill to swallow, for which I plotted retaliation during our production of *The Sound of Music* that spring. One night, I managed to sneak out of school wearing a nun's costume, wimple and all. My friends were in hysterics at my audacity, while the real nuns who taught us and were the bane of our existence, stood guard to ensure no one escaped. Nearly all of us had gone to Catholic schools most of our young lives and were less than enamored with the women in what we called penguin suits, who made our days miserable and supplied plenty of ammunition to incite this minor rebellion.

That night, we hopped into Candy's car and headed to a favorite hangout on the top of South Orange Mountain. Sr. Carol (that would be me) jumped from the idling auto, and while her friends circled the lot, marched into Gruning's to buy us a pack of cigs. Standing at the cigarette machine, which back then was standard equipment at restaurants and package stores, I slid the coins into the slot and pulled the knob for Newport. Nothing happened. I whacked the side of the machine again and again, like we did with our old TV, getting a little more violent with each attack.

At this point, a crowd was forming, appearing a bit befuddled at the sight of this aggressive nun buying the contraband of her community. Shrugging at them, I proceeded to the counter to complain about the problem. The checkout girl looked at me in disbelief. "I didn't know nuns could buy cigarettes," she said, as she handed me a pack of Newport's from behind the checkout counter. A mischievous smile spread across my face, as I snatched the pack from her grip, blurting, "No honey, they're not for me! They're for my friends," making a mad dash from the place, tripping over the tunic as I made my escape.

Next stop, my house.

My friends stayed in the car, the pack of hyenas that they were, still in stitches as I approached the steps to the front door. Pressing the bell, I glanced back at them as I waited for one of the parents who'd stolen my freedom to answer. A female voice, coming from behind the curtained glass door said, "Who's there?"

I responded with my best nun-speak, "It's Sr. Juanita, (my homeroom teacher) with some news about your daughter, Carol." But when I saw the look on my mother as she cracked open the door, I could take this prank no further. The blood had drained from her face as tears welled in her eyes. Only later did she tell me she thought I was dead.

There are no dramatic prom stories in my satchel of tales, as none of my close friends nor I went to the dance that year. Instead, we held up at Dotty's Short Hills' haven, where her Polish mom baked the best babka and paczki this side of the Atlantic, and where we got snookered on cheap red wine as Dotty impersonated Little Richard on her basement piano. The next day, we headed significantly hung-over to a beach at the Jersey Shore.

High school graduation is a blur, which says a lot.

I was eventually accepted to Seton Hall University, the same school my sister attended, and whose GPA allowed her to graduate magna cum laude near the top of her class. She was the oldest of us four, the star of the family, the good daughter who did nearly everything she was told. Children of alcoholics take on different roles, to survive the ordeal of feeling unsafe and abandoned in the dysfunctional setting in which they're raised. Her role, a second mom to the rest of us, is something I've been grateful for over the years.

My friend, Margaret, had told me about a girl named JoAnn, someone she'd met that summer, who she knew I'd like. Our first two years at Seton Hall were held in a dismal, old stone building in the heart of downtown Newark. The sweet smell of oil refineries was always close at hand. I pitched through the gloom and excitement of being in college and found this voluptuous Italian beauty the first day of classes.

We hit it off right away.

While I spent much of my time at home holed up in my room, avoiding the bitterness of my parents' bond, my weekends were spent with JoAnn, enjoying lavish five-course meals with her deeply Italian family, or hitting fraternity parties within a 20-mile radius of where we lived. At the time, we had gathered a circle of rowdy friends, some leftover from high school, some friends of those friends. Included in this group was a woman named Joan, known to set guys' pants on fire and to brush her teeth with a razor blade if she got too drunk.

One weekend, our basketball team was playing Boston College and offered a charter bus for students to attend the event. Joan, JoAnn, Janet, Louise, Betty and I piled onto the bus, screaming with laughter the whole way north. Joan had a nose for sniffing out rambunctious parties, where kegs and booze rarely ran dry. We'd hang on to the bitter end, when our dancing feet or ability to stand eventually wore out.

This particular party Joan uncovered was stockpiled with booze and drugs, and loud enough music to rock the street leading to the door. Mid-party, a SWAT-style team arrived. A mass of overly equipped cops in outfits akin to Darth Vader's poured through the door, with billy clubs attached to their fists. Kids scattered and screamed. Joan, snookered to the max, routed through the apartment, stumbling upon a window for us to climb through, with a battalion of open trash cans lined directly beneath.

Getting us out of harms way would literally stink.

Pushing and shoving our way to freedom, we took turns jumping, with Joan toppling into the most malodorous refuse in her rush to escape. She hauled herself out, spit on her hands, and wiped herself off, and onward we tumbled, roaring with laughter, to a party that lasted until our bus ride home.

After years of marching in the St.Paddy's Day parade as a high-school baton twirler, this celebration took on a whole new meaning in college. Only a short drive to NYC, we'd pour into someone's car, head to the parade, which was inconsequential, and stay most of the night. This year, six of us rented a room at the Warwick on the same floor as some bagpiping lads, and after eight hours of pub-crawling, we spent the rest of the night marching up and down the halls with them, bagpipes blaring, until finally getting kicked out of the hotel for our raucous behavior.

The following year, JoAnn and I attended the NJEA's Annual Conference in Atlantic City. As education majors, it seemed a fitting place to have some fun. After partying till midnight in the ballroom of our stately hotel, we headed to the bars. We picked up a couple of guys as the night charged on, ones who wanted to take us for a spin in their cousin's new Firebird, a fire-engine red convertible equipped with racing stripes down the sides. Buzzed enough to forget the frigid temps on this cold November night, we hopped right into the car. With its V-8 engine revving to the max, we sped down Ocean Drive, until out of the blue, this bright-red-bullet made a sharp left, zipping up the boarded ramp and landing us smack in the middle of the legendary boardwalk. Reaching a swift 60 mph, we hauled down the thoroughfare, hair whipping in our faces, whizzing past deserted taffy shops and ice cream stands that dotted this stretch of the renowned beach resort. JoAnn and I laughed so hard we peed our pants. Thankfully, we made it back to our room a little past sunrise, with no battle scars or arrest records to our name.

This time.

I must digress here, as events surrounding the Thanksgiving of my freshman year in college would have a huge impact on my life for years to come. My mom's sister, Lucia, with whom we shared alternating Thanksgivings for many years, came to our house with my Uncle Bill and their six kids for the family feast. It was the same year some ravenous cat devoured part of the 25lb turkey Mom had sitting on the back porch, which she called her second fridge. Uncle Bill refused to eat it.

He drank more instead.

After our formal dinner, where our parents imbibed enough not to care, the older kids, including myself, piled into my dad's red Plymouth station wagon for a trip to Long Island to visit my cousin's cousins. Aunt Lu had married Bill, a twin, whose identical brother, Frank, had a handful of kids we were going to see.

Lenny was one of those kids.

Lenny was my sister's age, with only one month between them, and always had a thing for her when our families got together. That is, until this weekend. After catching each other's eyes for most of the night, we stole away from the pack of cousins, still drinking beer and telling raucous jokes, and slipped into the laundry room, where his younger brother would grow massive pot plants one day.

We dove into each other's arms
our mouths like hungry pups at feeding bowls.

I'd had a few boyfriends in high school, a couple I honestly adored, one in particular who ditched me for a younger girl, and another I snubbed for the one who discarded me. One I'd someday regret snubbing. But at that moment in time, I was certain I'd kissed my soul-mate, or so my virginal body declared, who would drift in and out of my life for many years to come.

As children growing up, our summers were spent with these cousins on the hallowed Jersey Shore, with Aunt Lu and Uncle Bill's six, and Aunt Minnie and Uncle Frank's five. Lavallette, a small town wedged between Ortley and Chadwick beaches and named for the first rear admiral ever appointed by President Lincoln himself, was a favorite destination spot of our three families. The boardwalk that stretched from one end to other, with Seaside's amusement pier a short car ride away, made it the perfect place to vacation with families.

But that all changed in college. Belmar, with its brawny lifeguards and nightlife to match, was our summer town of choice. A crew of us rented an apartment directly across from Jerry Lynch's Bar and Grill, where we spent most of our time. After peeling ourselves off the beach with badly sunburned bodies, we were sure only a string of frosty beers would help us heal.

Jerry Lynch's had a semi-formal-ish bar upstairs and another raunchier one in the basement. The cellar bar circled the large rectangular room, with an upright piano situated in its center, where sing-alongs were held for mug raising revelers, till the bar closed its doors at 2am. Timmy and Danny were our favorite duo. There wasn't a tune they didn't know. They'd get the crowd significantly riled with classics like, *Roll Out the Bar-rel,* as mugs flew high in the air, clinking with your next-door neighbor's and spilling so much onto the floor, we were wading in it at night's end.

This is where I had my first depth charge, a shot of whisky dropped into a mug of beer, a ritual I embraced like the guys we drank with. We sat at the bar with shots and beers assembled before us, like raucous kids in lunch line, bought by the hoard of randy young men aspiring to hit on us at night's end.

Though we drank till we sometimes puked, most of us held on to our virginity, like the precious commodity it was. Years of Catholic schooling would do that to the most sex-crazed among us. One night, after flirting with the ever charismatic, Timmy G, during a nightlong sing-fest at Lynch's bar, I was invited back to his apartment for some post-work activity. Tipsy enough to accept his invitation, I found myself in bed with a man almost twice my age, one I only knew from his exuberant singing and flirtatious eyes. He wanted way more than I was willing to give, accusing me of cock-teasing, badgering me with ugly words that shamed me for the rest of the summer. I managed to escape date rape through a swift shove with my knee, but was further mortified the next time I saw him on stage with mic in hand, referring to me as that little cockteaser, warning the collection of men around me to stay clear.

Every time I returned to the club, he did the same.

My negligible self worth kept bringing me back

taking another nose-dive with each insult that spewed from his lips.

After a few of those humiliating encounters, we avoided him like the plague he was and headed for D'Jais, down Ocean Drive from Jerry Lynch's, where

Bruce Springsteen was known to hang, and the distinctive club to dance the night away. Our first night, "Lucy in the Sky with Diamonds" drifted through speakers with strobe lights spinning overhead, as shots of whisky and mugs of beer fueled our dancing. At the time, we were sure the Beatles were singing about LSD, and little did I know, I'd have my first and only acid trip a few years down the road, a night I'd like to forget.

As underage drinkers, we eked our way into bars with phony IDs. My brother taught me to convert an old driver's license, made then of heavy card stock and minus photos, into drinking aged identification. A razor blade and someone's discarded license could transform yours into a passable ID. I became the kingpin, upping the age of my friends to accommodate our increasing need to party.

And oh the places we'd go.

It was the summer of:

Crashing parties from Belmar to Point Pleasant

Yelling turtle mid-dance, landing on backs, feet up

Spitting small wads of paper through straws that stick to restaurant walls

Levitating bodies

Diving onto beds, missing them totally

Heads in toilet bowls

Tossing Oreos into toll bins in place of quarters

Launching off lifeguard stands, belly flopping on sand

It was the summer of grasping firmly onto a lifestyle of self-destruction that eventually became my downfall.

But in the meantime, I was determined to have fun.

chapter five

Heaving With Sobs

My sister quits drinking three weeks after I do. This getting sober seems to be contagious. She claims I gave her the courage to stop. Her husband will follow us the next year.

AA meetings become my new social life. I grab one of the little books, with a listing of the meetings close by, and memorize the ones I'll attend. My bashful self has re-emerged. I go alone to these meetings, held in church basements and rooms above garages, with smokers puffing away outside their doors, and huge pots of coffee always percolating on counters.

I stand in corners, scanning the crowd.

I see young people and old, who spill their guts, telling stories that make me laugh and sometimes cry. Screwing up some courage after hearing their tales, some with glimpses of my life woven through them, I gingerly approach these folks at meeting's end, to thank them and shake hands. Next time I come, I may even ask for their phone numbers to call them when I need support, because I'm really not getting it at home.

Besides telling my husband he has to come clean with me, our new therapist has insisted he end his affair. Apparently he does, because he spends his time moping around, playing songs by Roy Orbison on the stereo. I swear if I hear "Cry-y-y-y-ing" one more freakin' time, I just might kill him. While I grieve the loss of a lifestyle I once loved, he's grieving this other woman.

Of course, I don't know how to tell him this. He's always been the dominant one in our relationship. He's smarter than me, considerably more educated, and makes far more money than I've ever dreamed of making. He's a writer with a future, a future I'm unsure I'll be able to share with him. He sleeps down the hall now, something he's done for months since having sex with him became a chore.

We've started seeing our new therapist together, sitting next to each other on her office loveseat that squirms beneath us. It surely knows something I don't understand right now. We take turns blaming each other for what's gone wrong, you-ing each other to death, as defenses rise to a pitch that hurts ears. We don't know how to communicate any other way, as both sets of parents passed their dysfunction directly onto the two of us. Our therapist tries steering us in another direction, telling us to focus on ourselves, to "keep it in the I." I swear that I hear her, but quickly realize old habits are hard to break.

My sister, who's been living in Panama for 24 years, has moved into their Vermont log home for good. Forced to leave before the invasion in December, she calls every other night. She's a single mom now, caring for her teenage son, while her husband continues his ship pilot's job on the Canal. I try supporting her in every way I can, but know it interferes with my problems at home. My husband starts to complain. I love them both and don't know what to do. The desire to drink comes back. I haven't collected the phone numbers I told myself I would, and the craving overwhelms my days. I head out to a meeting when the yearning gets bad. My husband has issues with my need to flee. I think of the nerve he has, after all the nights we spent dining without him.

Our screaming matches scare our little girl.

She's the one you did this for.

She's the one who got you here.

She's the one you hurt the most.

One day he talks about leaving, and my hands want to reach for my ears, with my voice repeating la-las like our daughter does when she doesn't like what we're saying. Instead, I sink into the closet, sobbing like the five-year-old our child is, who witnesses this inevitable breakdown. My husband yells at me for this witnessing, which only makes me wail that much harder.

I don't know it yet, but I've been triggered, reliving all those months as a child, going from one family to the next, when my mother, through no fault of her own, abandoned me. I feel this abandonment deep in my chest, a chest that heaves with sobs, sobs I can't control, sobs that just keep coming the more my husband yells at me to stop.

The what-will-I-do-s march inside my head, the fear of being alone beats on my heart, bruising it so badly I think it might explode. My hand flies to my chest, in hopes of stopping the pounding that's now ringing in my ears. My nose is a faucet that can't be shut off, snot racing down my chin, slathering itself across my shirt.

My husband whisks my daughter from the room. She's now spilling the same kind of tears I find myself wading through. I can't begin to think about her, how her little heart must be breaking in two, that the same fear that surges through my veins, must also be surging through hers.

At this moment in time
you don't care a lick about her.
You have nothing inside but a minefield of fear
detonating with each new thought
that scurries through your brain.
You can't move.
You can't think.
You can't do anything
but cry.

chapter six

_____

Luck, and When It Runs Out

I lost my virginity between my sophomore and junior year in college, on the day my sister got married. She met her future husband at my parents' lake house, where that fateful party took place. Her fiancé was friends with a guy I was dating, who'd invited me to his homecoming at Notre Dame. It meant taking my first plane ride to visit him, aboard one of those 15-seat-prop-things I swore would tumble from the sky, with each jerk of turbulence that jiggled the plane. I drank away the weekend. Any torch I'd once carried for him quickly extinguished after those three slightly awkward, extremely intoxicated days.

It wasn't the last time this would happen.

My sister's wedding was held at the Merchant Marine Academy at King's Point, where her fiancé had graduated. Situated on the Long Island Sound, it was an ideal setting for this significant event. I was my sister's maid-of-honor and felt mixed about the whole thing, knowing I was losing my only sister to marriage.

Families and friends filled the chapel and following a tear-filled ceremony, with umbrellas in hands as rain poured from the skies, we briskly moved on to the reception, that portion of the wedding most people come for. Trays of champagne waltzed through the rooms, the glasses on them as tipsy as the revelers, disappearing far quicker than staff could provide. Hugs and kisses were consumed, while partygoers searched for place cards on circular tables, squeezed into these small but cozy rooms. My sister had hoped for a garden reception, but as champagne continued to twirl around the crowd, disappointments turned into letting loose.

I'd spotted Lenny in the chapel, pressed between his brothers, while walking down the aisle in front of my glowing sister. The tingling in my body had begun back then. By the time I'd had my fifth glass of champagne, it was spreading through me like rampaging electricity. I sought him out, every chance I could.

He'd been drafted a few months earlier and was waiting to be shipped off to Vietnam. We'd been writing back and forth since his deployment to Fort Meade. He'd be leaving in six weeks. My body felt an urgency it never felt before.

Though it rained the entire day, it didn't dampen the festivities. We drank and danced through most of the night. Plans were made during a lip-lock session in a neatly appointed restroom at King's Point to rendezvous at his parents' house, just 45 minutes away, to continue our semi-incestuous love-fest. I sensed this may be the night my precious commodity would be given away.

I was to sleep in his older brother Joe's room, only steps away from Len's, stashed in the basement of my aunt and uncle's home. That's where I started off, till we were sure most of the house was snoring. I then slid deliciously into his childhood bed, single and soft, where our bodies tangled, erupting in desire that would not be contained, where my deflowering took place on the night of my sister's wedding. He was gentle and kind, took my face in his hands, breathed love into my eyes, and entered me in a way I will always cherish. Six weeks later, he'd ship off to Cù Chi, and would come home a changed man.

After Len left, I continued to party, the only way I knew to deal with the pain of his departure and my sister's marriage. Abandonment was a major theme of my life, barreling through it like an angry rhino.

Deadened only by the drug of drink.

As I trudged through junior year, writing to Len became part of my homework. My bestie, JoAnn, had transferred to the University of Kentucky, and her absence was a thorn that was tough to dislodge. Sometime in March, I persuaded my mom to let me borrow her Rambler American. It was a funky green car I'd nearly crashed a number of times returning from fraternity parties late at night, back in the days when designated driver was a concept known only to a rational few. I was so blitzed on one of those nights, I saw double and covered an eye to make it home, the number of curbs driven over too numerous to count.

After much cajoling and begging, a technique I'd mastered as a child, my mother gave in, knowing how depressed I'd become from losing JoAnn. With brown paper bags stuffed with our change of clothes, my friend, Janet, and I headed west to Pennsylvania and Ohio, driving straight through the night, landing in Kentucky at the crack of dawn. JoAnn lived in a house packed with pot-smoking UK students. We had hushpuppies for breakfast, washed down with bourbon, then followed by a little more. In between, we ate pizza and smoked dope. Somehow we landed in the bathtub, with squeezeboxes and ukuleles to entertain us. We fooled around with Betsy, a Kentucky-style musket that we believed Davy Crockett had once stalked bears with, and cared little if it was loaded or not. We passed out on the floor and slept the sleep of old dogs.

My first real wake-up call (though others had banged at my door), came with a visit to Bethesda to keep my sister company while her husband was at sea. She drove north, fetching me in the VW bug they'd shipped home following their European honeymoon, and took me to a party where I drank lavishly all night. By the second night, the few gin and tonics I had produced hives from my chest up, tightening my airway, and landing me in the ER for Benadryl relief.

Surely a warning sign most would not ignore.

But this young emerging alkie blamed it on the tonic.

I'd had many warning signs prior to this episode as puking after a night out was a regular occurrence for me. Though it usually happened in the confines of our third floor bathroom, I remember a night of ingesting so much Southern Comfort on a date with some guy I barely knew, I puked out the door of his car five times. Ensuring he would never ask me out again.

In truth, it was my body's way of telling me I was poisoning myself.

My takeaway was to never bring Southern Comfort to my lips again.

That summer, my sister was invited to visit some college friends who had migrated to San Francisco after graduation. My cousin, Merry, and I were summoned to string along. It was the beginning of our ten-year relationship, following each other and whatever whim we had at the time. Merry, who's six days older than me, had been my cousin pal for years. We were excited about this adventure and would spend the summer with three of my sister's friends in a house where Clay meets Divisadero in the Pacific Heights district of this illustrious town.

We felt lucky indeed.

It was the summer of Janis Joplin singing live, only blocks from where we lived.

The summer of Fillmore, the summer of Santana and the Chambers Brothers, Canned Heat and Credence Clearwater Revival, Sly and the Family Stone and Ten Years After, to name a few. It was the summer of Haight Ashbury and Stinson Beach, of Sausalito and Golden Gate Park.

It was the summer of mopeds scooting up and down extravagantly steep hills. Of cable cars and winding streets.

It was the summer of that stunning orange bridge, under which I'd pick up the worst sunburn of my life, which made standing up in the back of a VW bug the only bearable way to get me home. It was the summer of playing bridge, chugging gin and tonics and lavish amounts of beer.

It was the summer of love.

One night, when our stash of gin ran low, after consuming enough to plant me on the back of a scooter with nothing on but a transparent raincoat, we dashed out for another bottle. We zipped around corners and stopped at traffic lights, where onlookers gawked, as I brazenly tossed them a wave. Streaking was becoming a common occurrence on college campuses and I felt like part of its tribe.

Another night, after downing shots of tequila at a local pub with guys we'd picked up hitchhiking after a weekend visit to Lake Tahoe, we were invited to someone's apartment to view *indie* movies with their friends. Near ready to topple over, Merry and I swayed in front of the screen, mouths agape, watching our first porno's with ten guys we hardly knew.

But the night I remember most was shortly after we'd arrived in San Francisco. We'd been drinking at a nightclub similar to Jerry Lynch's sing-along venue. My cousin and I yearned to sing the night away, and stayed behind after our group left, deciding we could manage the short taxi ride back to our friends' apartment. *We amn't intoxicated!* The bartender hailed us a cab, as we were in no shape to do it ourselves. We stumbled into the backseat, howling about something we'd done, reporting our misadventures to our doleful cabbie. He asked if we'd heard the news, as he turned the volume up on his radio, where somber words of Robert Kennedy's assassination, just two months after Dr. King's murder, tumbled through his speakers. Our giddiness turned quickly to tears, as we sobbed bitterly the rest of the way home.

At summer's end, our housemates crossed the country in a rented RV. Merry and my sister, whose husband was again out at sea, joined in the adventure. Heading into my last year of college, I was destined to fly home alone, missing out on their trip, and Len's arrival from Vietnam via SF by two weeks.

I would see him when he shipped back east, watched as he'd fall asleep mid-conversation, holding his PTSD in my heart, as he could detect an approaching helicopter before anyone else would even hear its sound. And that spring, I'd invite him to a wedding that would land me in the hospital for two weeks.

After JoAnn left Seton Hall, I became friends with Patty. An Irish Catholic girl from a large, close-knit family, I spent many nights cramming for tests at her home in Newark, and partying hard with her boyfriend and his fraternity brothers. They married before school got out that year. Their reception was held on campus, where we danced on tables, a favorite attention-seeking thing I liked to do, wondering why the reception ended so soon. While I was in San Francisco, my dad bought a Triumph Herald, a boxy, red convertible begging to be a sports car, failing miserably at the attempt. My brother and I shared the car, and it was my weekend to have our wanna-be sports coupe. Len and I decided to transport the celebration to my parents' lake house, where we could party in private. Len rolled us a joint and drove the Herald, as we bantered back and forth, looking forward to a night of intermingling. But as we approached a notorious curve-of-road faster than he or the car could handle, I found myself screaming, "Watch out!"

Len yelled back, "We're not gonna make it," as he lost control, flipping the vehicle over and over and over again. The man who witnessed the accident, who called the ambulance, who saved my sorry ass, was Sparta's police chief. He was certain I was dead, as I'd flown out the roof of that little convertible and landed on my head.

It was the one time being inebriated saved my life.

I escaped with a major concussion and a hefty subgaleal hematoma above my forehead, one that required evacuation by needle aspiration. When that mallet-sized hypodermic came at me, I let out a scream heard up and down the Jersey Shore.

They held me in the hospital for two weeks before seeing fit to send me home. Len called regularly and came to visit while I was there. I wouldn't hear from him for a while after that, assuming the guilt he felt for totaling the car and nearly killing me was huge.

I managed to catch up enough with schoolwork to graduate, but any cum laudes would not appear in my records. My eking by in high school pursued me in college. I was the hooligan, my sister the star, which persuaded me to skip graduation for the racetrack, invited by some guy I'd met at a bar the week before. I was my parents' worst nightmare, though they didn't seem to care what I did or how I did it.

They were lost in their own boozy haze.

One I was well on my way to joining.

chapter seven

No Dessert

I spend far too much time begging my husband to stay. His foot has been out the door for a while now. But I beg him anyway. I beg him when he rushes out in the morning, with coffee in hand and blinders on. I beg him when I call the college, imploring him to come home early, a petition he repeatedly ignores. I beg him at night, before retiring to separate rooms, where sleep seems miles away.

The stench of your desperation fills the house like garbage sprawling in open sun.

You beg until your voice becomes so weakened, your pleas turn to whispers.

Pleas that don't matter.

That fall on deafened ears.

If I'm not begging, I'm preaching. Spewing all the things they say at the meetings I attend. Things that even to me sound rather corny.

Things like:

Easy Does It

First Things First

What do these mottos mean?

Live And Let Live

Think... Think... Think

I already think way too much.

One Day At A Time

Let Go and Let God.

Let go of what?

Keep It Simple

Act As If

As if what?

And of course, one my mother used to say: *This Too Shall Pass.*

I'm not sure what these hokey sayings mean, but I preach them anyway. Each new phrase that spills from my mouth creates more eye-glazing in my husband. They say *keep coming back…it works if you work it.* I keep going back and though I'm trying my hardest, it doesn't seem to work very well at home.

They tell me to get a sponsor, which I go ahead and do, a woman a decade younger than me, who's been sober a couple of years. I dial her number when I dig up the nerve. She tells me to start the steps. I've already done the first, the one that took twelve years to achieve. Admitting I was powerless over alcohol and that my life had become unmanageable.

I'm exhausted at the thought.

When I see our therapist, I can't stop talking about my husband, all that's wrong with him, and how he wants to leave. She points me in a new direction, and suggests I attend an additional 12-Step meeting. Yeah, I'm that screwed up. It's one that's held on Smith College campus called Co-Dependents Anonymous. I'm incredibly desperate, so I give it a try.

A half hour in the room, I know this is a good place to be. I'm with a bunch of women just like me, who can't keep the focus on themselves. They use the term higher power here, which appeals to me more than God, a word that conjures up too many bad memories of my Catholic upbringing.

I go to these meetings every Tuesday and meet two women I click with right away. One of the women, who's working on a goddess calendar, will become a life-long friend. I love the idea of a female god and when I mention it to my five-year-old daughter, she says, "Mommy, everybody knows God's a boy's name."

The other woman has a son with special needs. I latch onto her like a barnacle on pilings. I don't know it now, but these women will carry me through my toughest times.

One that's right around the corner.

I'm preaching two programs now, and my husband can't stand another second of it, and tells me he's going to leave. I sob and beg, and beg some more, but it doesn't make a lick of difference. I tuck in my daughter at night and see my fear reflected in her eyes, and I tell my husband, "If you're the one who's leaving, you're the one who's telling our daughter."

One night after supper, after the table's cleared and dishes are done, after her bath is taken and jammies are on, the three of us situate ourselves at that maple table, in places we sit for dinner every night.

This time I know there'll be no dessert.

He tells her that he loves her and that he always will, "But Mommy and Daddy can't live with each other right now." I watch the tears pool in her eyes and feel mine doing the same. I can't look at him as he tells her he's found a nice apartment, in the next town over, and that she'll be visiting him there.

Tears that pooled now trickle down her cheeks.

A vise locks itself around my chest. I'm sure I can't breathe. I try taking in a breath, but little happens. I hear a wheeze. The asthma that gripped me as a child is making a visit. I try to calm myself, but I don't know how. Instinct guides me to pick up my daughter and hold her close.

Your breathing levels off
but not your husband's resolve to leave.

The next day, he asks, "What can I take? Can I have one of the Henckels' knives?"

"You mean the ones you bought me for Christmas?" I give him one, a boning knife he can use to stab himself with. I don't tell him that, but I think it, deeply. I give him the carbon steel knives I acquired when I worked at Frög.

One that I slit my hand with.

I give him the old junk I never really liked, and tell him to take everything that was his. I don't want to see his things hanging around the house, while the thought of losing them is unbearable.

Including the bed belonging to him and his first wife.

The one we slept in while making our baby girl.

And the day he plans to leave?

Is Mother's Day.

He leaves at noon
on Mother's
Day. You watch
the pick-up pull
away   the tarnished
brass bed   your con
nubial altar
now in pieces
exposed   for all to see
jostling in the flat
of the truck   as it
escapes
down the street.

Roaming the house   nails
bitten beyond the quick
hugging
your daughter   more
than she needs
you search
   for remnants
of the comforter
you called
   your marriage.

You gaze out
your bedroom window
daffodils blurring
in the spring breeze
   and realize
he must have
   taken that
with him
too.

* Lead poem from my chapbook, *DIVORCE PAPERS*

chapter eight

Freedom

With my sister stowed away in Bethesda, my best friend in Kentucky, and a boyfriend who seemingly disappeared, my mom felt sorry for me and booked us a trip to Bermuda. She and Dad had vacationed there when we were young and she longed to return ever since. She called it a graduation present, and even though my degree had yet to arrive, off we went to that tiny island some 640 miles off the coast of North Carolina.

The Reef was a resort not far from the Hamilton capital, right on a beach with fine pink sand and hoards of honeymooners. Every night at dinner, Mom and I clinked our wine glasses and watched them moon over each other at tables surrounding ours. We had a cute German waiter who shamelessly flirted with me under Mom's watchful eye, and invited me out for Bermuda nightlife, consisting of boozy beach parties around blazing bonfires with other hotel staff.

Each night, when Mom was tucking in, I'd steal away with Gerhard, the man who called me Sweet Orange, paying homage to the town where I lived. We drank from scores of bottles passed around the fire, till we fell into each other's arms, entangling our bodies till dawn. I crawled into bed a few hours before Mom woke and then slept on the beach, where we lounged and baked. I was grateful for the trip, my mom trying hard to hold onto her last daughter, though I had difficulty showing appreciation while we were there.

My drinking kept me trapped inside an emotionally young and self-centered age.

That summer, I retook the Shakespeare course I failed. Even after our island vacation, spending these months with my parents felt hellish to me. JoAnn was home from school and we bar-hopped most every night, never knowing who we'd end up with after last call.

I sent out job applications, not sure I even wanted to teach after a bad student teaching experience that awarded me a C, but interviewed for the New York City school district in July. When asked if I was any relation to Al Weis, the Mets second baseman who let a playable ball go through his legs with loaded bases in the 24th inning of a game that spring, my flippant response was, "Oh yeah, he's my husband," which basically sealed the deal.

He blew the game and I blew the interview.

And then the saving call came through from my cousin Merry. Aunt Minnie and Uncle Frank were moving out of their house and leaving it to the kids. We were packing up and heading to Long Island to join them.

This was the home where Lenny spent his childhood. Where I'd lost my virginity a couple years before. Since coming back from Vietnam, he'd moved in with a fellow vet, 20 minutes from where I now resided. Of course, I chose his old basement bedroom to move into, with cousin, Merry, in the room next door. Len's sisters, Antoinette and Kathy, shared another bedroom upstairs, while his brother, Ed, and his wife, Lana, slept in the fourth. Len would often stay over, sleeping on our couch, as his affections for me dialed back since the accident. My moving into his parents' house caused suspicions of desperation not well hidden at the time.

There was always a joint being passed around, and though this was not my first experience with pot, I was amazed by its inexhaustible supply. We were never without it, and smoked every night over games of knock-hockey on the just-been-cleared dining room table, or dealing hands of bridge with jugs of cheap wine to moisten our lips. We smoked it through the Mets' first World Series, hooting and hollering with the rest of their euphoric fans. I was getting the college dorm experience I never had, with people I loved. One endless party, night after night, with one of the funniest guys I've ever known.

Ed was the middle child in his family, and like me, dealt with his emotional wounds by becoming the clown of his clan. Though his mom hardly drank, his father made up for it ten times over. Having five kids, three of them boys in a span of four years, would lead many to say he deserved to. Everything Ed said was funny. And Merry and I were his favorite audience. We'd howl till our cheeks hurt, till we couldn't laugh a second longer.

A month or two after our arrival, he got a call from his college friend, Rickey, inviting him up for a weekend in Syracuse. Lana had to work, so Merry and I went along for the ride. It was the first time I'd meet my husband-to-be. A tall stringbean of a man, with a glint in his Irish blue eyes, he was getting his M.Ed. at the university that shaped his philosophy of education.

We played the weekend away, with pot and beer our constant companions. *Abbey Road* had recently been released, which spun until the record wore thin. At one point, in the wee hours of morning, splayed like dogs across the kitchen floor, we whacked empty beer bottles like hockey pucks on the checkered linoleum. The four of us were in wasted hysterics, until, one by one, we each fell into intoxicated sleep, as inebriation took possession of the game. Our weekend ended with a snowball fight at Cayuga Falls, where Rickey stole a kiss in the backseat, as we drove him back to his apartment.

I wouldn't see him again for another nine years.

In the meantime, I was introduced to another friend of Ed's. Patrick was also a Vietnam vet, who was known to many as Potty, and had a twinkle in his eye that latched onto mine. A student of the streets, Pat had stories up the wazoo, and took a liking to me on our first meeting. Little did I know, that twenty years down the road, he would end up a strung-out crack head called Captain Zero, wandering the beaches of Costa Rica with his pack of motley dogs, escaping prosecution for drug smuggling, and the center of a book by his friend, Allan Weisbecker.

Pat introduced me to hashish and the pleasures of Ditch Plains campgrounds, with its all-encompassing beauty, near the outermost reaches of Montauk. We spied on Dick Cavett, who owned a house on the cliffs and walked his dogs on the beach below, cliffs that towered above the ocean where Pat loved to surf. We partied with Truman Capote and his band of splashy friends, guzzling gin and tonics under the awning of his silver camper, with Chinese lanterns dancing about beneath the starry Montauk sky. We shagged the night away in

Pat's orange pup tent, with his ever-present dogs looking on.

Since Pat was a wanderer, I also spent time partying with his friend, Don Byrne, another casualty of the Vietnam conflict, who vied with Pat for my affections. Don would get so bloody wasted, he'd pass out mid-sentence. I remember a night in his basement, where he literally conked out while having sex, a definitive slam to this girl's fragile ego. A few years later, when I was living in Philly, my father informed me of his demise, falling onto railroad tracks I could only assume in a drunken stupor, where an oncoming train instantly killed him. I always wondered if it was intentional, his wounds from the war too hard for him to bear.

While in Lindenhurst, I signed up for my breakout venture into substitute teaching. My first assignment was a class of eighth-graders, who filed in and out of the room in waves of chaotic motion. Arriving home, still shaken from the experience, I guzzled five successive glasses of wine, not nearly enough to calm my thrashing heart. I quickly turned down every new subbing assignment offered me.

Instead, I accepted a position at Scudder Avenue School, two towns over in Copiague. Since I was without a car, I bought myself a zippy little motorcycle. It was a red Honda 90 reminiscent of the bike that scooted us around San Francisco, which I buzzed to work on, and to various bars at night.

That I never crashed that baby was a major marvel.

One weekend that year, Ed, who was giddy with excitement, asked Merry and I if we wanted to drop acid with him. He had scored some squares of Windowpane, a variety popular at the time, and wanted to take the train into the city especially for the trip. I was all on board, while my cousin had her doubts, but agreed to accompany us for kicks. As we stood at the station waiting for the train, Ed placed a translucent square on his tongue, like a host at communion, then one on mine, and tried to persuade Merry to join us. As she hemmed and hawed, giggling at the thought, Ed slipped the pane into her mouth. Merry was coming along, whether she wanted to or not. She would end up having a mind-boggling time, as I clawed my way through a night of psychedelic hell, having a classic bad trip, as endless hallucinating was not my thing. Being in New York City is a trip all by itself, but on lysergic acid diethyl-amide, it became a nightmare of onerous proportions.

The drug kicked in at Penn Station, where we sat on the floor for what seemed like days, as ordinary people floated by, their faces melting into each other, distorted from ear to ear, reflections of horror-show-mirrors brought to life.

Colors blaring

flashing

changing

bleeding into each other

hands sinking   into the floor   I sat on

while my brain morphed to liquid

sloshing inside my head.

Beside me were Ed and Merry, laughing their asses off as this circus paraded before us, enjoying each nano-second of this bizarre reality that sent me reeling. *I've gotta get out of here* splashed through my brain, as they fell over laughing at each weird form prancing by.

At some point, Ed, a man of great appetites, declared, "I'm starved," and wanted to find a place to eat. Glued to the floor, I shook my head vigorously at the thought of going anywhere but home, believing my brain would pour onto the pulsating flooring if I shook it any more.

We headed for a two-bit diner Ed knew of on 31st Street, as each step taken, a walking freak show unfurled. People were stretching, shrinking, and melting as they oozed by us, a Dali painting come alive, and while Merry and Ed impersonated hyenas, my palms dripped, as our morphing faces reflected in shop windows increased my heartbeat to an off-the-chart rate.

We ordered breakfast as dawn and walls closed in and by the time plates slid onto the table, the diner had become an oven and strip-off-clothing hot. With my earlobes about to burst from heat, I pushed back my chair saying, "I gotta get out of here," longing to rip off my clothes as I stood. Merry and Ed took a few more bites and led me home. I finally came down five hours later.

The trip stayed with me for months, even years. I'd walk down the halls of school with kids coming at me in slow motion, their faces distorted into gremlins and ghouls. Smoking pot became a chronic anxiety for me.

At the time, it was more important to fit in

to be one of the guys

to be cool and liked

saying no was not a word I could easily utter.

A problem not painless to overcome.

One night while partying with Pat, he suggested we trip on some hash-laced pot he'd scored. In other words, smoke enough to trip out like on acid. He was charming and persuasive, and before I knew it, I was deep into that nightmarish hell once again.

It would take years for me to change this kind of behavior.

To take care of myself just by saying no.

With some, it takes a sledgehammer.

chapter nine

Staving Off Pain

My daughter crawls into bed with me.

Something she does every night.

She can't stand the thought of being alone.

Neither of us can.

A ritual we do to stave off the pain.

The first time she goes to her dad's, he calls me around 9pm. "She won't stop crying," he says. "Can I bring her home?" I sense a familiar feeling on a shelf in my heart. It's the same thing I did when my mom went to the hospital. I haven't discussed it in therapy yet, so the only tangible sign is the tightening in my chest.

A slight wheeze escapes as my eyes swell with tears and I whisper, "Of course. Bring my baby home, right away."

He carries her into the house, with her face blotched from weeping. Her arms reach out to me, as her breath catches with sobs, the look in her eyes shredding my heart. "Mommy, Mommy, I missed you too much," she whispers through her tears. I carry her to bed and cuddle close. I never want to send her there again. I know I'll have to. But the thought rips me to pieces.

You long for a drink.

You need to call your sponsor

but the grip she has on you right now

is unmovable.

I fill the void of sobriety by calling old friends, ones I know will understand. Ones who can sip the same glass of wine all night long. My mother, of course, doesn't get it. "How could you be an alcoholic?" she says. "You didn't drink that much, did you?" All the friends I drank with think the same. They're surprised I've stopped. *Why would you ever do such a thing* teeters on the tips of their tongues, longing to be shaken off.

My sister-in-law is delighted. She always worries about my brother's drinking. The one who used to drink alone. Who'd pour a glass of Scotch from our father's cherished bottles and drink by himself, when no one else was home. I felt sorry for him when he told me this, remembering my mom saying that he would sneak into the backseat of my aunt and uncle's car when they came to visit. They were the parents he knew, the ones who took care of him while our mom was hospitalized the first time.

I'm grateful for his wife's support. She sends me greeting cards like I've graduated from some prestigious university, with the magna cum laude I never achieved.

I've merely graduated from the hell I ran from for years.

I call my cousin, Paul, Merry's oldest brother, the one who's been sober for a while, who I used to avoid when I drank. I yammer on about my husband. I can't help myself. My focus is still on him. Without hesitation, he tells me the order of things. "Now that you're sober, *you* need to come first in your life. Then comes your daughter, and lastly your husband. It's the only way you'll stay clean." He talks about his life, how happy he is, having gotten married in November.

You wince at his words.
You can't bear his happiness.
You endure it for his wisdom.

I go to meetings every day. They tell me to listen, that it's the newcomer's job, but it's taken me five months to finally speak up. I have so much garbage inside my head, I need to take some of the trash out. It feels so good to be honest with myself, as I proclaim out loud, "Hi, my name is Carol. And I'm an alcoholic."

I bring my daughter to meetings, dragging along her yellow sleeping bag with orange ducks waddling around it, and the Barbie dolls her dad buys for her. I grimace at their presence. Coloring books and crayons are more to my liking. She lies across the stage upstairs in Easthampton's town hall. Wrapped in yellow, she colors pictures of Ariel, as well as Beauty and the Beast, next to the tables where I spill my pain and listen as others spill theirs.

The noon-er in Noho becomes a favorite of mine, where throngs of drunks fill the basement of the UU church, with the smell of coffee floating through its musty air. My daughter sits on my lap, as too many folks scout around for available chairs. They glare at five-year-olds who take one of theirs. I listen as she squirms, holding her tight as drunken tales drift around the room.

I meet a woman whose story resembles my own, who tells me about a meeting in Holyoke, a city where I rarely go. She says it's packed with old timers and their wisdom is like gold. The next day, we head for that meeting. It's held above an auto body shop on High Street, in a small green room on the second floor, with two rectangular tables huddled by folding chairs that fill up the space. As we climb the decaying stairs, creaking loudly as we ascend, I wonder if this is a good place to bring my daughter. It looks more like a site to score drugs than gain recovery. But I peek in the room and sit down anyway.

A woman named Trina, with frosted hair and a voluminous voice, speaks of her husband who scares her to no end. For some reason, she annoys me, but she's always there. So are Ted and Alicia. She's disabled and I hardly understand what she's saying. But her kindness shines through her strained speech. Ted has recently relapsed, but is trying again.

Then there's Walter, the eldest old-timer. He's going bald and parks himself at the head of the table like he owns it. No laughing from this man, as many do when they recognize themselves in what others say. I hang on carefully to his words, the ones that drip with the wisdom that many years of sobriety bring. He intimidates me, his sternness reminiscent of the nuns I had in school, but I listen with the reverence he deserves. The woman who told me about this group is there. She smiles as I give my daughter the brown bag lunch I've packed, yogurt and carrot sticks, a box of raisins, and some juice. I know she has a daughter. She understands. While Trina, who I end up becoming dear friends with, wonders why there's no chips or soda in that sack.

I become a regular at this gathering.

Like Trina, I can't stop talking about my husband. I talk about his drinking and how I wish he'd stop. I blab about my love for him, though it feels more like hate, and share my uncertainty of working things out.

Your voice quavers with the words
as tears rush to your chin.
Your grief lies prostrate on the table you sit at.

I go on a date with my husband, to some unremarkable movie I can't re-member, a safe place for us to go. He gives me my support check, which he does weekly, and comments on the way I talk. Remarking on my saying *you know* too much. "You should try and break that habit." I listen to myself stum-bling through the night. Every sentence I utter, starts with *you know*, putting knots in my stomach, the kind sailors tie.

And I wonder if I'll ever get it undone.

I try undoing this behavior
but like my relationship with him
it seems I'll never get it right.
No matter how hard I work on it.
I'll never get it right.
Instead, I cut off my hair.
To an inch of my scalp.

chapter ten

Deux Vins, S'il Vous Plait

During my last month as the Title 1 Teacher at Scudder Avenue School, we received a flyer listing discounts for educators who wanted to travel to Europe that summer. The $115 round-trip fair to London was hard to resist. I brought the flyer home and after an exuberant discussion, Merry and I were heartily on board. We booked two seats on a charter flight out of Kennedy, leaving at 7:30pm on June 30th, with $200 a piece in traveler's checks that would last until we flew home from Amsterdam on August 24th.

Before starting this adventure, we agreed to have sex with obliging men in each country we'd visit. The sexual revolution had taken hold. And we knew our proclivity for inebriation would see us through this lascivious goal.

We sat at Kennedy for hours, visiting the bar closest to our gate. Our flight was delayed and we filled the anxious moments with what we did best. By the time we clambered aboard the plane at 2am, we could barely see through the haze of excitement and booze.

We arrived in London, mid-afternoon, backpacks stuffed beyond comprehension, sleeping bags atop their bulge, with no idea where we'd spend the night. Ending up on the floor of Victoria Station, cross-eyed and haggard, leaning against our ginormous rucksacks, we considered sleeping there. Our savior came in the guise of a 73-year-old man, who had a flat with an extra room, not far from the station, where we could sleep for 30 quid. We shrugged our shoulders, slung on our packs, and followed him home.

We slept in a room thick with dust and shared bath water the next morning in a rusted and dingy claw foot tub (reminding me of the beauty my sister and I had in our third-floor bathroom), as we gagged at the smell of breakfast our host was making. "You girls eat fried eggs and tomats, dontcha?" he warbled from the kitchen, as hands held over our mouths kept us from vomiting all over his bathroom floor. We politely ate breakfast in his tiny kitchen, each bite taken suppressing the urge to retch. A jar of soured lard, the stuff that flavored our food and assaulted our senses, sat atop the counter nearby. We quickly paid for our room, grateful for the kindness, as we'd slept more than 13 hours in his dust-laden guest room, where I sneezed through most of the night.

Eager to hit the road, we took the train out of London, disembarking closest to the M1 entrance that headed north. Still exhausted from our long day before, we quibbled about how to catch our first ride. Spotting a petrol station, I approached a distinguished looking gentleman gassing up, and asked if he'd give us a lift. His name was Sydney Orchard, a James Bond-ish sort of guy, as the car he was filling was a Rolls Royce. He gladly accepted our request and we hopped in his Rolls for the ride of our lives.

Every 50 km or so, we'd stop at a pub and Sydney would proposition us, insisting we stay with him for the summer, saying all our expenses would be taken care of. We'd laugh, get back in his white sedan, and off we'd go again. At one point he let me drive; going 100mph in a Rolls Royce was like riding on velvet. Sydney dropped us off in Sheffield, realizing we had too much adventure ahead of us to stay with him, where we picked up a lorry ride to Windermere and the first of many youth hostels we'd sleep in.

The next day, we hitched north to Scotland, through Glasgow and up to the Highlands' Isle of Skye, the largest of the Inner Hebrides, which other hostelers urged us to visit. Amazed by the northern lights, a place where postcards got written in daylight at 11pm and time meant little, we stayed on Skye for four days, soaking in its peace. The beauty of Scotland was particularly breathtaking, the pubs crowded with people we couldn't understand. One couple picked us up hitching and to everything they said, we'd laugh and respond, "Excuse me?" Until the man finally stopped the car, turned, and spit out, "Don't ye damn Yankees speak English?"

One of our most memorable rides came south of Edinburgh with a man named Malcolm, who claimed to be a model on his way to a photoshoot. He was fraught with worry about having a weak portfolio, and would we mind helping him out. Before we knew it, Malcolm was turning off the highway onto a rutty dirt road through a Scottish field of tussocky grass, stopping a half-mile or so from the main thoroughfare. Unbeknownst to us, Malcolm had nothing on under the beige London Fog he wore that day. He whipped out his Polaroid camera and off came his raincoat, asking if we'd take some shots of him to fill up his folder.

Hung over as we usually were, partying hard in Edinburgh the night before, we shrugged and took turns with his Polaroid, taking shots of Malcolm in the nude, as his pecker grew larger with each photo we took. We became so invested in the project, we actually took pictures of each other posing with Malcolm, arms wrapped around waists, souvenirs of our trip to share with our families back home. Malcolm, who'd promised a much longer ride than he delivered, got a flat tire the minute we returned to the highway. As Malcolm fumbled with the jack and dealt with his karma, we stuck out our thumbs for a lift back to London.

We connected with Lana and Ed, who'd taken a later flight over, and partied with them for a day or two before parting ways. Ed had rented a motorcycle to escort them through Europe, as we chose a more adventurous means of transport. Before leaving London, we visited my artist cousin, Carl, and his wife, Jeremy, who introduced us to bangers and mash, and hearty ale in their Soho studio.

We also met up with a group of guys who worked at Apple Studio. Of course, they knew The Beatles, which elated us to no end. They'd worked on a few of their albums and were there for their rooftop concert, telling us stories that regretfully, my drunken mind couldn't hang on to. They took us to a party in a flat above the Studio, where bongs were passed and liquor flowed freely. Two of these men were our first European conquests. We'd stay with them the night, dreaming of being with John or Paul, and were booted to the street the next day.

Our last night in London, we rolled out our sleeping bags in Hyde Park, discovering it was illegal when a copper woke and informed us of it in mid-sleep.

We charmed him into letting us stay the night, then hitched out of London the next day. Heading for the White Cliffs of Dover, we caught the Hovercraft to Calais and on to Paris, where the real challenge began. Our four combined years of high school French did little to help our cause. The two things we could easily say were, *où est la salle de bains* (where is the bathroom) and most importantly, *deux vins, s'il vous plait*, which slid off our tongues with ease.

By the time we reached Paris, our backpacks had grown so cumbersome, we decided to ship home some clothes. Doing so made us homesick and the only cure we could think of, aside from going home or getting drunk, was attending a local showing of "Woodstock," which had premiered the week before. Both of my brothers had attended the concert the previous summer with Merry's younger brother, Steve. I peered longingly at the scenes, hoping to spot their sweet faces, the ones that annoyed the heck out of me for so many years. We sat there in tears, long after the moviegoers dispersed, huddling close in this unfamiliar Parisian theater. We got a taste of what home really meant, though still early into our European adventure.

We stayed in Paris a few days, swilling wine and visiting the tourist spots we always wanted to see. Each morning we chugged strong coffee to wipe out the cobwebs of too much vin, and munched on baguettes as we strolled the historic streets.

Heading out once again, we traveled to the towns where our rides were going. And while most tourists sipped the wines they ordered, we guzzled ours. One glass of Chablis was never enough, and we gleefully drank our way through France, with hangovers our morning greeting.

We crossed the border into Spain, and were dropped off in the heart of San Sebastian, which curls affectionately around the Bay of Biscay. After finding ourselves a cheap pension, we basked on the beach during the day, and hit the clubs at night. After partying till dawn with a couple of studly Basques, we slept on the white sandy beach, turning every few hours to even out our sunburns. We slathered each other with lotion, then stuck out our thumbs for our next ride.

We moved on to Madrid, in the heat of summer, with temps soaring over 95 each day, making hitch-hiking less than desirable. Since we'd sent most of our clothes home, laundry was always in order. After settling into the hostel, we made our way to the laundromat, garbed in mini dresses we rarely wore. A young Spaniard, maybe 9 or 10 years old, scampered by and lifted the back of my dress. Much to his surprise, he found a panty-less bottom, as I was washing all the other clothes I had with me. We howled about this with hostelers we met going out at 11:00 that night, the only cool part of the day, then stayed in bed till hangovers wore off.

Barcelona was another hot city, where we swooned over paella and drank our first pitcher of sangria. One pitcher turned into three, and when we finally crawled into bed, our pension room spun wildly. Waking again at 3am, we were both so hot, the only way to cool off was by taking cold showers, returning to narrow beds naked and sopping wet.

We eventually hitched north to the Costa Brava to a small town called Costa del Mar. Staying a few days, we drank wine around campfires, swapping stories, singing Leonard Cohen songs with English-speaking hostelers. Little did we know, we'd see him in concert the following weekend.

July quickly turned into August, and with much more to see, we headed north. We were picked up by three guys traveling toward Aix-en-Provence for a three-day concert that would rival our own Woodstock. "You have not heard of this?" they asked in their French-laden English. We hadn't, but knew it was where we'd spend our weekend. Arriving on Saturday, we snuck into this festival, as funds were dwindling and rebellion was our badge of honor.

Imagine Woodstock, with a slightly smaller crowd and all announcements in French, and an audience from who knows how many different countries. Topless girls in bellbottom jeans, arms raised to the heavens, twirled about. Hash pipes and fat joints passed from group to group, with bottles of vin ordinaire in everyone's hand. Helicopters tick-tick-ticked overhead, as a string of chanting Hare Krishnas weaved through the crowd. When Leonard Cohen rode onto the stage atop a white stallion, the crowd went wild. Johnny Winter, with his flowing white hair, brought down the house. But it was Mungo Jerry's *In the Summertime* that gathered the most screams.

Everyone was up on his or her wasted feet, dancing wildly.

We stayed up most of the night, squatting in the dark on makeshift toilets—slabs of boards above a deeply dug trench—holding our noses, praying we didn't topple in. After hours of chugging wine and warm beer, shagging who knows who and when, we then trudged along with the odiferous crowd, as concertgoers streamed from the grounds. Our thumbs went out as usual, and we were picked up by a couple of young Frenchman who'd also been at the concert. They pulled a Malcolm-esque maneuver, turning off the main drag onto a dirt road that wended its way through a field of un-harvested wheat. Bringing the car to a halt, they turned, and in a mishmash of Anglo-Français said, "Flirty-flirty, cinq minutes, cinq minutes?"

We must've had fools stamped across our foreheads, but laughed it off as we did most things, and replied through slightly uncomfortable giggling, "Non, merci."

Their voices became more aggressive, faces tight-fisted as they repeated the same asinine approach, this time with a heavy-handed tone, "Flirty-flirty, cinq minutes!" We laughed some more, shaking our heads, as I elbowed my cousin, indicating it was time to escape. Before we even threw our backpacks out the doors, the engine revved, as these indignant Frenchmen abandoned us to the deserted field. Hungry, exhausted, hungover to the max, but grateful to make it out unscathed, we meandered back to the main drag, sticking out our tired thumbs once again.

At the onset of our trip, my cousin and I agreed to take turns sitting in the backseat. The person upfront had to converse, while the one in the back got to sleep. This day was filled with magnanimous lorry drivers, where we both sat up front and had to chat. Our rides that day took us into Lyon, where we found a hotel so cheap, the landlord emphatically declared, "Ne bain, ni douche!" (no bath or shower). By then, we were so tired, we hardly had the strength to do either.

The next day, after sneakily bathing from a sink, we made our way into Switzerland and landed in Geneva, surrounded by snow-capped mountains and nestled on an alpine lake, its beauty beyond compare. We were picked up by a man named, Stefon, who took us to dinner at a classic Swiss restaurant where we sat fireside, dipping chunks of crusty bread into vats of melted Gruyere, our first excursion into the goo of fondue. He ordered a bottle of Williams Pear Schnapps and when that was finished, ordered some more. He lured us back to his apartment, where he promised us couches of our own, but spent the night hounding my cousin, as squeals of, "No, Stefon," accompanied by intermittent slapping sounds rang through his modest apartment.

We both woke with grade-A hangovers, the worst we ever had. Packing our things, we hit the road, heading toward Chimonix at Stefon's suggestion, and were quickly picked up by a German family driving into the Alps for a weekend of mountain climbing and family fun. They asked if we'd like to join them. We shrugged our aching shoulders, and said, "Sure, why not?"

We drove up into the mountains, with peaks too high to see, each curve we took, making our hammering heads throb that much more. When we saw the terrain we'd be traversing, we wondered what we'd gotten ourselves into. One glance at the wooden clogs I'd successfully worn since leaving New York over a month ago, I sensed I'd be in more trouble than I cared to imagine.

But we were tough and made it up the mountain, huffing and puffing through each tenuous step we took, with edelweiss dancing at our feet and views of Mont Blanc's glacier but a stone's throw away. We stayed the weekend with this dear family, picnicking on German wursts and hearty brown breads. We dangled our feet into alpine streams that could only stand five-seconds of dipping toes, as we watched hardy Germans swim in the same.

We were sad to say goodbye to this adopted family, who kept us sober for those three rugged days and eventually dropped us on the outskirts of Munich, where we aimed to rectify that unreasonable condition. Turning francs into deutsche-marks, we hit the first biergarten we could find and dove right into German brew. Too tipsy and tired to find a hotel, we rolled out our sleeping bags in the Englischer Garten, a park within city limits that became our home for the night.

The next evening, we stashed our stuff beneath a bush we hoped to easily find, and hit the Hofbräuhaus, one of Munich's notorious tourist traps. Coming from German ancestry on our mothers' side of the family, and my possessing a name as German as could be, we knew we were in our element. We ordered steins as tall as our arms were long, drinking far more than we should, which was always the case. That night, we met a young man named Gunther, who thought we were funny, and invited us back to his flat. It would take awhile to track down our packs and sleeping bags, but with Gunther's help, we found the stash and followed him home.

The next day, hangovers included, he insisted on taking us to Dachau. We ambled through the grizzly museum, with his guilt at being a German following us around, pouring from this young man's soul like rusty water from an old faucet. "But it wasn't your fault," was repeated over and over, until its triteness wore thin, words that Gunther could not take on as his own. I think we were still saying it as we hugged him goodbye.

We ventured north to Darmstadt in hopes of collecting mail, and doing three-week-old laundry while there. We waited a couple of days, and since no mail arrived, headed for Hamburg, where we lifted mugs on the shores of Alster Lake. Having less than two weeks left of our travels, we were heart set on getting to Copenhagen to visit my mom's friend, Angie Novello, who'd been Robert Kennedy's secretary for 15 years. She chose to leave the country following his death, and was now secretary to Angier Biddle Duke, Ambassador to Denmark. My family had visited Angie in Washington when I was 12. She'd shown us around RFK's office, who regretfully was out of town, and took us through the hidden tunnel to the Capitol where deals are proposed on the run.

We were eager to pay our respects to this historic lady.

We stayed in a hostel overnight, then hitched north to Fehmarn, an island with ferry service to Denmark. And sadly, where Jimmy Hendrix performed his last concert just three weeks later. We arrived too tired and late, and slept on the beach close to the ferry slips, rolling out our sleeping bags on fine sand. That night, the fog rolled in along with the cold and we shivered in our bags, huddling close to each other to try and stay warm. The steins of beer we imbibed at a Puttgarden pub contributed little to the cause. We woke still shivering, soaked from fog so thick, we could barely see anything but each other through its dense curtain.

We slept on the ferry to Rødby, and as our thumbs went out for a ride, we were swiftly picked up by a charming Dane named Eigil Knudsen. He lived just north of Copenhagen and persuaded us to stay with him for a night, which quickly turned into three, as he treated us so kindly and spoke the English we sorely missed. We made a call to Angie, who wouldn't be able to see us till then.

Each morning, we woke to a smorgasbord of food covering his dining room table, a Danish tradition we immensely enjoyed. At night, he took us to Tivoli

Gardens, its fairy tale lights twinkling around us, where I drank till I puked, hogging the stall to the displeasure of ladies in line behind me, as fireworks erupted overhead.

The next day, we toured the countryside and rode horses at a stable Eigil frequented. Finishing our day after downing bottles of Tuborg, we stood beside a pier, where water thick with jellyfish mesmerized us with their undulating dance.

Eigil drove us into Copenhagen for our visit with Angie, where we stayed the night. We sat with her for hours, sipping wine, listening to stories of her years with the Kennedy clan, tales only a close family member could tell.

With only a few days left before our flight back home, we made our way to Amsterdam, and rolled out our sleeping bags in an arcade with a bevy of young travelers. Sleep was almost impossible, as joints and bottles were passed around, a fitting way to end our adventure abroad. Though we missed a few countries on our proposed sex-a-thon, we left Europe with a deep friendship that would drive us through our 20s and 30s.

Until I made the significant step to end the madness.

chapter eleven

Tip of the Anger Iceberg

My husband takes one look at my hair and can't seem to hide his disdain. He wonders if I'm turning gay, with all the women I talk about when I'm with him. I've always had women friends—ones who supported my drinking, who shied away when I stopped—but never like this.

They are my scaffolding

while I paint a new me.

I've reached Step 4, the one that says to make a searching and fearless moral inventory of yourself. I'd start writing stuff down if I had a clue of what that means. My sponsor fills me in on character defects and my takeaway is all the bad things I say about myself inside my head. And things I may have confessed if I were still going to church.

I'm so frickin' desperate to patch up my marriage, I skip to step nine. Making amends isn't hard for someone who says I'm sorry far more than she should. So I meet with my husband first, though I honestly believe he ought to be making amends to me. I apologize for my nitpicking and my obsessive control in the kitchen. For putting him down in front of others, which seems to make me feel better about myself.

I don't mention withholding sex.

It's the one thing I'm not sorry for.

Not now, at least.

I was told not to expect anything when making these amends. That people respond in different ways. There's a reason they say this. I still have in the back of my mind that this may prompt him to apologize to me. I'm dead wrong about that. My husband says thanks, that he appreciates my doing this, but wonders why his friend, Ed, who got sober before me, has never done the same with him.

He cares more about that than he does about me.

I still feel lost most of the time, and though I haven't been to church in who knows how long, I wonder if going back might help with the lost-ness. Since my husband lives in the next town over, I think it might be good to try St. Mary's, near where he lives. I get our daughter all dressed up and meet him there on Sunday mornings. The three of us sit up front, so our daughter can see what's going on. Although I think it might be a sin, something I don't much believe in anymore, I have a crush on Father Dave, finding comfort in his sermons. The rituals and smells of the church I was raised in equally console me.

We also get invited to a family party. All the cousins will be there. My husband can't go, but I decide to take my daughter anyway. And I wonder if I need to make amends to any of these kinfolk.

My therapist advises me to just have fun.

We ride the ferry to Long Island, feeling sad as we cross the sound alone, and spend the weekend at Aunt Minnie and Uncle Frank's East Hampton home. My cousins, Merry and Liz, recently had their first babies. So did Len, who married a woman 25 years younger than himself.

The news of it spreads like wildfire through the family grapevine.

"Can you believe it?" is always attached to the gossipy leak.

These cousins I used to drink with are still in the game. Except for Ed, my partner in sobriety. I find myself judging as I watch them all imbibe and a wave of envy splashes over me, as I guzzle club soda, while they quaff their wine. The next day at the beach, Maggie downs cans of orange soda she never gets to drink at our house, and throws up in the cooler as we drive through the night heading home.

Her head is in the toilet till the break of dawn.

I find out later she's not the only one.

The chicken salad Len made was tainted with bacteria.

You try not to be giddy when you find this out.

As this would be your last family reunion

for a number of years.

The discomfort of this event leads to another.

We make plans for Maggie's birthday. Rickey suggests a pool party, held in the town where he now resides. I decide to invite my mother, a mistake I'll live to regret.

She's used to my old lifestyle, where drinks flow as soon as dinner hour draws near. "Why can't you just have a little wine?" she says. Discussing drinking with my mother always turns into a skirmish. So instead of going into why I can't have a little wine, I tell her how happy I am now that I'm sober, that the burden of knowing and hiding my problem has gratefully been lifted. "But can't you have a little wine? One glass can't possibly hurt." She doesn't get it and never will.

I know she's been drinking, as a quart of vodka is stashed in her suitcase. I've already gone to the guest room to check. Even though the knowing will drive me crazy, I find myself doing it anyway.

Old patterns die hard.

I've invited a handful of Maggie's young friends and we meet Rickey at the designated site. I bring a chocolate cake I baked for the occasion. One the adults like, but not the little kids. Rickey brings hot dogs and burgers, and a cooler full of beer. He offers one to my mom. They laugh, these two who rarely get along, and become allies in the war against my sober self.

I feel like I might explode. Eventually I do, not caring who hears or what they think. The kids playing in the pool all stop and stare. I feel my face turning red, but all that rage my drinking pushed down, wants to come out and shake its fist.

You walk away

and burst into tears.

You'll soon find out

it's but the tip of

the anger iceberg.

The least little thing seems to set me off. I send myself to my room quite often, so I won't take things out on Maggie, the innocent one. The one who came to me, to get me sober. My therapist suggests I write things down, and I start keeping a journal of my thoughts and feelings. The anger flows from pen to page in forceful strokes; my inability to write lyrically is frustrating. I'm becoming aware of how I see myself, always comparing myself to my sister, always thinking I'm the stupid one. Maybe I should go back to school. It might help me discover who I really am. I'm in search of a proving, mostly to myself, but also to the world at large.

The journaling seems valuable, but the steam of rage keeps coming out of my ears, like a pressure cooker ready to explode. I need to take a run, more than I did before. One day, I'm ready to take off, and Maggie, who's playing dress-up with my old clothes, begs me not to go. Obviously, she can't see the steam and tries chasing me down the street, clip-clopping in three-inch purple heels, tears running down her cheeks. "Mommy, come back," she cries, as the anger pushes me forward, yearning to ignore her pleas, but my heart splits open from the sound of her pain. I stop and wait, holding out arms and picking her up, purple heels dangling from the ends of her feet. I carry her home, the two of us crying, still spilling our grief, a faucet that flows when it damn well pleases.

Each time my sister calls, I feel annoyed, though I never tell her directly. I make snide remarks like I've always done, ones that slither out the side of my mouth, but aim straight at the heart. I need to make amends to her, but I'm not quite ready to do that. Instead, I start to pull away. At some point, I realize I don't have to pick up the phone. My answering machine will do it for me. I can screen calls, and only answer when I feel up to talking. I don't do it often, but when I do, I tend to piss people off.

And you think to yourself
in the back corner of your subconscious
let them feel how you've felt
all these miserable years.
Though you're not really sure why you did.
You haven't gotten to the meat of things in therapy.

chapter twelve

The Kiss of Death, and Other Nonlethal Adventures

Merry and I settled back in with our cousins in Lindenhurst, but found the wanderlust too tempting to resist. While spending a weekend camping at Montauk's Ditch Plains, we were picked up hitching into town by a sweet guy named Vinnie, who worked the front desk at Gurney's Inn. After explaining the hotel's need for extra help, we decided to stay in Montauk, and hang our backpacks up at the inn.

A rustic resort located on Old Montauk Highway, Gurney's Inn languishes beside the sea, admiring the view of the pounding surf. At the time, it was owned by Angelo and Nick Monte, who we swore had mafia ties as John Gotti was one of its frequent guests. This inn became our on-and-off home for the years of our early 20s.

We were hired as chambermaids by a young woman named Linda, all prickles and glare, who took a liking to us and our carefree ways. She'd suck in her cheeks, trying hard not to laugh, while reprimanding us about being late or improperly folding sheets. Setting us up in the dorms, my cousin and I shared a room above a boisterous kitchen, where food was served to us three times a day, enjoying meals with the multicultural staff who were here on working visas, some expiring soon.

When we weren't working, we hunkered down at Shagwong, a cozy and somewhat dive-ish old bar in the center of town, where celebs like Andy Warhol and the Rolling Stones hung out, and that served the best french fries in town. We became regulars, where people knew our names, chucking our shoulders and drinking tap beer with us, until the last call arrived just before 2am.

This often compromised our duties as chambermaids, a job that fit perfectly into our blithe way of living. On those really bad days, when hangovers ruled our world, we'd climb into the beds we were paid to make for a quick recovery nap, praying the occupants wouldn't return while we snoozed away morning headaches. More than once, we'd rinse glasses in toilets we'd just cleaned, having already wiped down the sinks, not wanting to duplicate that particular job.

We hung out with a diverse crew of foreigners, relishing the sundry accents they used telling tales of why they came. Fernando, a busboy from Colombia, had aspirations of attaining his green card to stay in the country where dreams were made. Mark, a waiter from Ireland, as cute as his accent, would nightly relinquish his kitchen duties with the tag line, "Time to go Wishbone, time to go," was saving money for school. And the handsome Marion, a native Jamaican, would be the first Black man I'd ever sleep with.

When we weren't at Shagwong, we'd be at Salivar's, a dockside bar nestled amongst fishing boats in Montauk harbor, alongside piers where Pat bought bluefish for our Ditch Plains' dinners. It's where the fishermen drank, where the preserved head of a 4,500 lb. great white caught back in 1964 by Frank Mundus (whose *Jaws'* character Quint is based on), smiled ruefully as it hung over the billiard table where we played pool. It's where we met Roger McCann, both fisherman and pool-shark, and one of the most unhinged men I'd ever know, who, one night, nearly choked me to death with his calloused hands.

We played pool for beers and won more than we lost. We'd bank shots the guys often missed, handling the bridge like Minnesota Fats, until we were too tipsy to chalk the stick or see the cue ball. We prided ourselves for lasting as long as the guys, drinking some under the tables and closing the bars down, then hitched home to our dormitory room. The designated driver was a thing of the future, and we often drove home with someone worse off than ourselves.

We became friends with Elliot, who was care-taking the estate that Peter Beard would buy in a couple years. One of the buildings was an old windmill, perched on a cliff overlooking the sea, a half-mile or so from Ditch Plains. El-liot was an impressive cook and prepared feasts for us, featuring fish he'd fetch at the early morning docks. Baked striped bass was often the star, swimming in a sea of onions, sculpted carrots and tourné potatoes, floating in the driest of whites, sweetest butter, and fresh picked herbs. Washed down with endless bottles of wine. Afterwards, we'd strip down to skivvies and sizzle in the sau-na, sweating off the alcohol we'd just tossed down.

And of course, another good reason to drink some more.

We drank with gusto and verve; always the thing to look forward to at day's end, never understanding the underlying causes of this ritual we had wrapped our lives so tightly around. We followed in our parents' footsteps. It was our way of being, and theirs, and like our parents, living without it never crossed our minds.

Of course, drinking stripped us of our Catholic school inhibitions, the ones the nuns spent years ingraining into our souls, resulting in sleeping with every Tim, Rich, and Henry that drifted into our nights. Oftentimes, we'd have sex with the same guys.

Fernando was one of the men we shared. A gentle and thoughtful spirit, with a rich Colombian accent, he was more attracted to my cousin, but would regularly settle for me. At one point, I agreed to marry him, to help him obtain his green card, after my cousin turned down his proposal, fearing she'd be locked in with a man who cared for her too much.

It was a time of illicit ideas. I became a shoulder surfer, memorizing others' calling card numbers while listening from the next booth, then using those numbers to call home, claiming things were fine, longing for an air of respon-sibility, while pulling it off in a delinquent manner.

We stayed in Montauk for almost a year this time around, but as winter closed its shutters, dragging us down to the depths of its bleakness, we yearned to go south. We bought ourselves a VW Beetle, a bright blue one with a clutch-less manual transmission, filling it up on the first leg of the trip for a measly three dollars and fifty cents.

We drove straight through to Georgia, until our eyelids could no longer stay open. Pulling into a rest stop with potties and picnic tables, we rolled out sleeping bags and slept on top of the wooden slabs where people ate. I distinctly remember being stopped by a Georgia cop for what seemed like no other reason than our northern-plated car, carrying two wide-eyed twenty-three year olds, heading south for the winter. This particular cop hailed straight from pervert city, lumbering towards the car with his Bill Gillespie swagger, then leaning in the window with a lecherous sneer. "Now whatch you sweet little things doin' in a town like this?" We swore we'd memorize this town, whose name I forget, and never pass through it again.

We made it to West Palm Beach late the next afternoon and were told, "They're looking for help at The Breakers, just across the bridge in Palm Beach."

The Breakers was a sprawling old-money resort with its long horseshoed driveway lined with dancing palm trees, and filled with the glitz and glamour Gurney's Inn lacked. We knew we were out of our element, but got hired right away in the dining room, this time as roll and relish girls. We took turns carrying hot aluminum boxes strapped to our chests. Filled with fresh dinner rolls, we served them with little sterling silver tongs to diners with coifed hair and dripping with jewels, who inhabited the hotel. If we weren't doing that, we plopped gherkins and dill slices on their classic side plates.

We boarded in side-by-side rooms, tiny cells similar to those novitiates are given. We stuck our heads out the windows above our narrow single beds to chat with each other, dishing about this extravagant place where we were working.

At night after our shift ended, we hit the local bar, a flashy nightclub on the hem of the resort. It was where we met Sam and Henry, transplants from England and line cooks in The Breakers kitchen, who spoke in the accents we admired most. While other women ordered Singapore Slings or Tequila Sunrises, we threw back shots of tequila and beers, heading back to our tiny rooms with spinning heads and slurred speech.

One night on our way to the bar, we saw a valet we'd come to know take a brand new fire-engine-red Corvette for a spin before parking in the lot where it belonged. We watched as he spun out of control, zipping down the 20mph service road at what looked like 60, totaling the car before our very eyes. Witnessing that required a few extra shots, as we were shaken almost as much as him.

Any excuse to drink a little more was always welcome on both sides of the bar.

When the season ended and workers moved on, Henry and Sam headed west to Las Vegas, while Merry and I veered south once again to camp on the legendary Keys. We dropped off our friend, Puna, a Hawaiian girl and waitress at The Breakers with lava-black hair so thick she could tie it in a knot without using pins to hold it in place. This thoroughly amazed these sandy-colored-fine-haired cousins. Our last time seeing her was at a rowdy bar in Miami, where revelers danced to *Sympathy for the Devil* in daylight, woo-wooing the afternoon away. We dove head-first into the festivities and woo-woo-ed right along.

We set up our little orange pup-tent on various sites along the Keys, camping on this no-see-um portion of the state, until reaching our final destination on this otherworldly string of islets. By the time we arrived in Key West, we were crispy skinned and eager to party.

Key West was yet to be known for its sunset celebration, though word was spreading, where artsy folks and buskers gathered on Mallory Square Dock, celebrating the end of another day. We were fascinated by this ritual and by the people who showed up. A juggler, a magician, a sword swallower, and clown. A tightrope walker and sad-faced mime, and a lone bagpiper whose melancholy sound seemed to help move the setting sun along.

We bumped into guys who knew Montauk and Pat, surfers following the waves, who took us to a string of bars, then back to their grungy place. We crashed till sunrise, where surfboards and empties were the main décor, sleeping with surfers past the wee hours of dawn.

We eventually drove back north, spending another summer at Gurney's Inn, where we moved in with Vinnie, to one of the cottages the Monte's owned. Vinnie was a pet of the owners and had privileges we never possessed. He scored this beautiful house set on the hill on Webster Road. with its working fireplace, a view of the sea, and bedrooms of our own. Though mostly like college girls who put up with roommate-sex on a regular basis, we were glad for the privacy this housing provided. I'll never forget the night, after a number of beers, I cracked an egg into Vinnie's Italian leather slip-ons, an incident he'd both scream and laugh about for months to come.

Our time at Gurney's was filled with celebrity sightings and tales. We were assigned to Jimmy Breslin's room, where he worked on one of his novels, with his typewriter and desk overlooking the ocean. His fingers raked through his hair, with each interruption we made when knocking on his door to deliver spare soap or towels. After slacking off for the day, he invited us over for beers, ordering a slew of bottles from room service. The two of us hid in the bathroom when the beer arrived. So taken by us, he moved to an offsite cottage, so we could spend the night eating pizza and drinking beers with him. We listened to stories of his defeat with Norman Mailer, who ran for mayor with Jimmy as city council president, an idea he said Gloria Steinem came up with. But the city decided they were too rowdy to hold down the jobs, and their plan of making NYC the 51st state, went down with them.

One night, after visiting our aunt and uncle in East Hampton, we stopped at a bar in town and sat in a booth directly behind Dustin Hoffman. From the conversation we leaned close to overhear, we figured he was chatting with his therapist, discussing intimate details we could vaguely make out. As we were leaving, the wise-ass that I was approached his table and stuck out my hand, saying, "I heard you wanted to meet me before we left." He smiled slyly as I said, "My name is Carol Weis, and it's nice to finally meet you."

The conversation went on, as he kept repeating my name, "Carol Weis, Carol Weis," shaking his head with recognition, wondering where he may have met or seen me before.

I flippantly replied, "Oh, maybe sitting in some theater, watching one of your fabulous films." With that, we made a dash out the door, holding our stomachs and howling, having punk'd Dustin Hoffman, way before it became a show.

During our stint at Gurney's, I met a man named Tim Clark, an entrepreneur from Chicago who came to Gurney's quite frequently, and had a huge appreciation for the amount of alcohol I consumed. Tim would get so drunk, and though this was a hard thing to accomplish, I'd actually get embarrassed being in his company. One night, while we were out to eat at a fairly decent restaurant, he asked the server if we could change our seating to a table that didn't wobble. When the waitress handed him a pack of matches to put under the off-kilter leg, Tim lifted our table, and proceeded to switch it with another.

He invited me to go canoeing with him, up through the Lakes District of Wisconsin and into Canada, this man I hardly knew, and of course I said yes. We were dropped off by train onto some wilderness river where we started a weeklong journey, portaging from lake to lake, camping without a thing to drink, never seeing another human for five straight days. We ended up losing our canoe in a set of rapids, grabbing our packs before the boat sank. We made our way back to the train tracks and hitched a ride on a handcar, the three of us motoring the wrong way down the track, anxiously listening for trains coming from the opposite direction.

I was an adventure seeker, an adrenaline junkie, who sought the rush and the numbing that went with it, then craved the drug that would counter the gust. The first thing we did when we got off of that handcar was look for the closest bar.

Sometime after returning from my canoeing escapade, we lost our house with Vinnie and were moved to another on Second House Road, where my cousin and I were forced to share a room again, a spacious one on the third floor, with eves we hit our heads on every time we sat up. The only saving grace was its easy access to the nightspots we patronized. I became involved with Roger, who both intrigued and repulsed me. A fisherman by trade, he'd traveled to many exotic places I'd only dreamed of going, doing stints on large fishing boats that trawled South American coasts. He also drank and swore like a sailor—the words that flung from his mouth would surely have made my mother cringe.

One night after an evening at Shagwong, where I'd declined his advances to sleep with him, he started following me home, angry at my refusal, a duty he mistakenly assumed I possessed. The night felt darker than usual, and as I turned onto Kirk Park trail, I picked up speed as he lurched after me, cursing me out, "You fucking cunt," as he drew near, and when he finally caught up, he grabbed me by the neck and thrashed me around, coming far too close to choking me to death.

Alcohol.

The definitive cause for this frightening event.

Fishermen seemed to draw us in, and after years of living in Montauk, we finally found one willing to take us out for an excursion. We'd stayed awake much of the night from the Irish coffees we drank, often our late-night choice to keep us going, this time robbing us of the sleep we'd need to go on this adventure. We slept at the fisherman's home, so he could wake us before sunrise to deliver us on time for the charter's departure. Bursting with excitement, nausea from the previous night's shenanigans came over us both, before even climbing aboard the vessel. My cousin and I only lasted a half-hour or so with a fishing pole dropped over the side, when seasickness took hold, retching into buckets as onlookers shook heads, until we were safely back on solid ground.

Lesson learned.

Never go fishing after a night of Irish coffees.

We stayed at Gurney's through fall, and one notable day when the sun was glaringly bright, red and rusty leaves rustling around us, we laid hung-over in the backyard of our Second House cottage. With our 25th birthdays closing in on us, we somberly declared we had nothing to show for our lives, making us nothings, *absolute* nothings. The notion made us laugh, as most things did, and we howled till our cheeks hurt at the thought of our nothingness and all it implied.

We left Gurney's soon after, my cousin heading home to south Jersey, with me going back to Lindenhurst, to linger until I had some fleeting notion of what I wanted to do with my life.

One night after my return, my cousin, Kathy, and I took a trip into the city, a quick train ride away, for a night on the town. We met two men, Sal and Hy, who were twice our age, at a nightclub somewhere on the Eastside of Manhattan. They bought us drinks and eventually persuaded us to return with them to Sal's apartment for a nightcap. One drink led to another, and before long, with lights dimmed, we paired off and were snuggling in our respective corners of the small quarters. Destiny lured me to the couch, where I cuddled with Hy. In the midst of sloppy smooching and freely roaming hands, eyes closed in a haze of liquor and lust, my arm, stuck under my companion's back, grew numb. Upon moving to reposition myself, I heard a thud, specifically a body dropping to the floor kind of sound.

Hy had fallen off the coach, just like that.

I rolled my eyes and snickered, while *jeez, this guy passed out mid-kiss* staggered through my mind. Hopping off the sofa, I straddled his fully clothed torso, gently smacking the sides of his face. "Come on, Hy! Wake up!" With no response to be found, the smacks grew vigorous and more pronounced, as I amped up the volume of my voice. "HEY. HY. WAKE UP!"

That's when I felt the dampness, inching its way around my thighs.

"Eww!"

I jumped up and switched on a light, disturbing the canoodling duo on the opposite side of the room. "Oh my gawd, you guys, I think he might...."

My cousin, the nurse, composed herself then rushed to check on his status, and immediately noticed the liquid staining the crotch of his pants. "Oh god, I think he's...," then went on to explain how a bladder empties itself when a person dies. My hand shot to my mouth, squelching the gasp that was dying to escape, as my cousin knelt beside him, pressing two fingers to the side of his neck. "I can't get a pulse." As she placed her ear to his chest, tears gushed from my eyes, while a torrent of shame shouted guilty as charged!

"Call 911," she screamed, as she started pumping his chest. Sal didn't budge, so she repeated, "Call 911. Now!" with a voice loaded with all the command I lacked, as I slumped on the sofa falling apart.

After making the call, Sal paced in that hand-wringing sort of way that makes onlookers extremely nervous, and then suddenly announced, "You girls, you gotta get outta here." With that, he gathered our purses and shoes, rightly perceiving I was in no condition to do it myself, and whisked us toward the door. Fear flickered in his eyes as he scanned the apartment. "I gotta find that damn gym bag before the cops come." My cousin and I eyed one another, wondering about its contents. Could it be drugs? We knew the implications of finding illegal substances on the premises, though I could barely see through my haze of tears.

My overly composed cousin slipped on her shoes, whipped out a pen and scrap of paper from her purse, scribbling our phone number and then stuffed it into Sal's hand, beseeching him to call with updates on Hy's demise. But when the doors to the elevator slid open, we both realized at the same time we couldn't leave.

We suspected something was up and returned to the scene of the crime.

Sal was not thrilled to see us. "You girls shouldn't…" but my cousin pushed him aside and strolled in. I took one look at Hy's body and wailed. A knock closely followed. Sal's agitation was off the charts as he peered through the peephole. A slew of cops poured into the apartment, firing off questions like a semi-automatic. The EMTs confirmed Hy's death, slipping him into a body bag, while I sat at the kitchen table and bawled, guilt in full control of my tears.

The cops stood around and laughed, smoking cigarettes, questioning us for what seemed like days. My cousin did most of the talking, as the only words that slipped through my lips were, "What's so funny?" and "Is Hy really dead?" When they finally let us go, Sal walked us to the elevator, pressing bills into my cousin's palm to catch a cab to the train.

We rode in silence as dawn cracked open the day, wondering if they'd found the gym bag, and what it contained. My cousin still hadn't shed a tear. That would come three weeks later in the dead of night, ignited by a nightmare she suffered in the middle of a fitful night's sleep.

Kathy graduated from nursing school that year and we celebrated all night long. Staying up was a common practice at that seemingly invincible time of life. But the next morning, something happened that changed all that. Sitting around the dinning room table, hungover to the max, eating a breakfast Aunt Minnie had made, I stood and started singing in my opera-style voice, something I often did to liven things up. *A Hard Day's Night* was the day's tune of choice, but mid-song, something snapped inside my head. A switch was flipped, and I was back inside my freaked-out-acid-trip, experiencing a full blown panic attack that lasted the rest of the day.

Little did I know, it would continue for nearly a year.

chapter thirteen

Slashing the Cord

I sign up for a course at a local college, the one where my husband also teaches. And one I know quite well from the many times I've dropped by to visit
him there. I need something to fill in the hole where drinking once dwelled.
The course I take, _The Influence of Play Upon Young Children_, is taught by a
woman I know from The Good Table, a breakfast place I frequented with my
husband when I still drank. My professor, who is lively and kind, introduces
me to picture books I fall deeply in love with. I read them to my daughter,
from the list she recommends. _Miss Rumphius_ takes the lead. That little girl
inside me, who doesn't recall ever being read to or the closeness this ritual
provides, snuggles a little closer every night.

In therapy, I talk a little about my childhood. I open myself up to the angst
of that time when my mother left me in the care of other families.

Abandonment.

The key source of all that pain.

Carrying this home, I feel it seize hold when I head off to class, as leaving
my daughter in the care of another suffocates me. It stirs up feelings that booze
helped to subside.

I feel myself slipping into resentment, resenting the fact that I've given up
something that relieved so much pain. I hop on the pity pot, the one they talk

about at the meetings I go to. The pot my expanding butt and attitude get stuck in and can't seem to pull myself out of. My lips rattle off complaints, ones I don't think I can possibly resolve. I feel myself sliding off the cloud I've been sitting on. The coming of winter squeezes out the last hints of pink in that puffy, once cozy nebula.

You turn to sweets for comfort.

Chocolate becomes your food of choice.

I get news that Uncle Frank, Lenny's father, has passed away. The uncle I grew to love and visited often when I lived in Montauk. After he had his stroke, I went to his house in East Hampton to do PT with him. Following our sessions, we'd clink glasses of whisky, drinking to his health.

Everyone will be gathering for the funeral.

Everyone, that is, but me.

Your sadness fills your heart, but will not change your mind.

You cannot face all the booze that will be poured after his service.

You'll be talked about on the family grapevine for years to come.

I notice my daughter scratching her back and find patches of scaly skin around her waist. I can't believe I'm just seeing this now. Too much time on the pity-pot can do that to a mom. I take her to the doctor, who says it's eczema. Guilt follows me out to the car, for passing my allergies onto her.

The ones I picked up when my mother was sick.

My guilt turns into resentment, like everything else.

I notice, too, that the care of the house is slipping away. My husband once told me his first wife was a slob, while earnestly hoping I wasn't like her. He had little need to worry about stuff like that. My fear of abandonment kept me in line. But now that he's gone, keeping a spotless house is last on the list of things I must or care to do.

That is, until Christmas swings around and he comes to celebrate with us. I break my back to get the place clean. Since our usual ritual of Christmas Eve champagne has been shed, and as one bottle was never enough, the tension swells the air with strain. It's the kind so thick you could slice it with a serrated knife and serve it warmed with slabs of butter at dinner.

My daughter's friend and her younger brother, who live down the street, come to celebrate with our family. Their military parents are loading C-5s for Desert Storm. My husband feels sorry for these kids and makes our daughter, who's already opened her presents, give one she just unwrapped to the little brother. His pity for him overtakes his fatherly concern for her. She screams and cries, spilling the grief we all feel this day. This jumble of desertion licks its chops, right there for all of us to see.

As I still go to meetings everyday, I head out after Christmas dinner, leaving the mess for my husband to clean. I go to a movie with him on New Year's Eve and see *Misery,* which seems to fit the mood of the night. It's the anniversary of my last drink, one I'm glad not to be celebrating. But New Year's Day is a different story. I sign up to speak, qualifying in front of a roomful of drunks, and share drunken tales with people who care. They give me a coin that I'll cherish for years. *To Thine Own Self Be True* is inscribed around its edge.

You've been sober one full year.

Clicking heels instead of leaded flutes.

I leave the tree up longer than I should. Various decorations lounge around the house for weeks on end. My daughter has taken a liking to the nativity scene, the stable and figurines I placed strategically on the toy chest cornered in the family room. Like everything else, it cries to be put away. One day, I see her playing with Mary and Joseph, holding them in a way that seems unfitting for these religious figures. Mary is yelling at Joseph, as he waits his turn, then yells back at her. The voices sound remotely familiar. I feel a cringe rising up my spine, and wonder how many fights this poor little girl has witnessed and absorbed.

It's my husband's weekend to have our daughter, so I go to a movie by myself. For the first time in my life. I see one playing at the Calvin, a theater that drips with history in Northampton. It only charges a dollar to watch a first-run film. On this night it's *Silence of the Lambs*, one I know little about. I buy myself a bucket of popcorn to eat while I'm here. I scoff down the kernels, shoving fistfuls into my mouth with each new horrifying scene. Though I can't wait to get out of there, I stay till the end.

I race to my car, glancing over my shoulder every second or two, checking the back seat before I climb in. Getting home, I search every closet in that big old house, terrified to stay in it alone.

Especially without the comfort of a drink.

I finally fall asleep, relieved that my dog is lying on the floor, slumbering quietly next to my bed.

This year, we spend Mother's Day together at my husband's place, a dramatic difference from last year's debacle. We start out by going to Mass, this newfound ritual that for now comforts my soul. Our daughter wears her new yellow dress with puffy sleeves and lacy fringe, the one her dad bought with her for Easter a month ago. My heart seizes up when I look at her. My husband even cooks for us, almost making up for last year's departure. We spend the rest of the day with him, taking pictures of me playing outside with our daughter.

My hope soars like the yellow in her dress.

I watch too much TV to fill the long lonely nights. The news sets me off more than it should. I become obsessed with the Clarence Thomas hearings. Anita Hill takes the stand, sharing her story like they do at the meetings I go to. I immediately identify with hers, as a switch gets flicked inside my head. The anger I've squelched over all those years, all that harassing and mistreatment I let myself endure, begins to seep out. One night I get so mad, I lock the door to my room. An explosion's about to take place and I fear my head might pop right off with it.

If your daughter comes into your room right now
the back of your hand may just swing her way.

I bring the rage to my CoDA meetings, where women like me are as fed up as I am. I begin to embrace the feminism I never fully valued when I was young, back when Betty Frieden penned her book. I tell my mother and my sister, who don't really get the whole feminist thing. I try and explain that keeping a house and raising a kid is an admirable calling, but it just isn't enough for me. They can't understand me turning my back on the way they've chosen to live. My anger offends them, though my mother has felt it much of her life.

You start to pull away from them
You stop the calling
And stop taking their calls

You know they'll hold you back
Back from the anger you need to release
Not only for the unjust world at large
But the anger you feel towards them
They have a psychic grip on you
You need to slash the cord.

chapter fourteen

_____

Angst Rises in Revolt

After that initial panic attack, I went back home to live with my folks. The familiarity of its comforting aromas settled down my terror for a day or two, until it erupted again. My mom felt sorry for me, which curbed the anger she usually spewed. She was glad to have me home, assured me each morning things would get better, though she was mostly at a loss for how to help. Her knee-jerk way of showing comfort consisted of food, the sight of which made me feel sick.

In a few month's time my weight dropped 20lbs
while fighting my way out of this frightening abyss.

I spent most of my moments sealed in my room, curled in the bed I grew up in, the only place I felt safe in my childhood home. Friends came to visit and I could only spend an hour or so with them, sitting in the confines of my parents' living room.

Before my palms begin to sweat

      heart pounding at racetrack speed

eyes shifting   this way   that way

        heart pounding faster faster

can't breathe   can't breathe

             gotta get outta here

    need to run   need to run   need to run

losing my mind…

I'd have to excuse myself and dash upstairs to my bedroom, certain I was going insane, until things settled down, and I could breathe again.

Racing thoughts dominated my nights

making sleep improbable

which added to the cycle of panic.

My sister and her husband had moved into a house two towns over, in Millburn, which soon became my *newest* home away from home. She'd recently had another baby and amusing her kids seemed to slay back the panic that was ruling my life. That is until the next attack occurred, the fear button pushed again, locking me into a state of sheer and utter terror, afraid I was going crazy and would never find my way back to sanity again.

A few months prior to this rampage of fear, I'd read a book called, *I'll Never Promise You a Rose Garden*. A novel based on the author's own life, it described the mental breakdown of Deborah Blau, a teenager who was eventually hospitalized for her psychological disorder.

As I tossed and turned at night, I pictured myself in restraints, tied to a gleaming metal bed, white sheets soaked from sweat in some *Snake Pit* of a hospital. A straight jacket waited in the wings, with madness screeching around me. Though it was summertime, I'd wake up shivering, in sheer dread of the upcoming day.

I didn't drink for a good six months. The mere smell of alcohol nauseated me. But spending time at my sister's where a bottle of wine was always around, poured to take the edge off long days with two small kids, I eventually slid back into its warm embrace.

My panic attacks diminished a bit as time went on, but were frequent enough to make employment impossible. My sister was friends with a guy working in social services, who recommended a psychiatrist named Dr. Campbell, someone who could prescribe medication to help me sleep. My mom had given me her Librium, similar to the drug the Rolling Stones sang about in *Mother's Little Helper*, which helped calm me down. I wanted more of those, or something similar, as Mom's stash was running low. Instead he gave me six Dalmane, to ease me back into a regular sleep pattern, which knocked me out nicely.

Six was not enough.

Dr. Campbell seemed competent, all stuffiness and business as he sat across from me in his cushy chair. But when he asked me, "Do you suffer from titi-tis?" I was a bit skeptical. Tititis? Could this possibly mean what I thought it meant? "You know," he continued, "have you ever worried about the size of your breasts?" I looked down, catching a peek of my slightly more than aver-age-sized chest and said no.

But really, what's it to him?

I talked about my parents, how their incessant fighting dragged me down.

"They don't get me," I said. "My mom's always mad and they put me in the middle of all their fights."

"Their fighting binds them together," he said. "This is the way they relate. Without the fighting, there'd be no marriage." I believed him, because I was young and clueless, and had no one else of his stature or prescription pad standing in my corner.

I chattered on about college, "I was such a lousy student. I have a degree in education, but I don't really want to teach," then I ran down the litany of jobs I'd tinkered with—babysitter, file clerk, chambermaid, short order cook, sales clerk, Title 1 Tutor—and how clueless I was about what to do next.

Especially since I had so much trouble just leaving my room.

I rambled about relationships with men. "I fall for all the wrong guys, you know, like my cousin's cousin. I've loved him since I was 12," I said, "and since I had sex with him, I just feel confused, like my heart may jump outta my chest."

"I see," he said.

He asked about other men in my life, boys really, and I plucked off a list, the ones I chased and who inevitably ran away. "I don't understand why this is happening," I said, though I never told him how I was abandoned at three. That my mom was sent to a sanatorium after my brother was born, with tu-berculosis attacking her lungs, and I've been a needy little kid ever since, leav-ing claw marks on the backs of all the wrong men I've picked.

I didn't have a clue back then.

He never once asked about alcohol, the disease that ran in my family like an overgrown grape vine. He needed to know this critical tidbit, but I never said a word. On my last session with him, he grandly summed things up by stating, "It seems you feel ineffective in three crucial areas of your life: with your par-ents, finding a career, and most certainly, your relationships with men."

I agreed with him
and proceeded to get up and carry that proclamation
into the rest of my life.

At some point during my stay at home, feeling desperate for financial inde-
pendence and well enough to look for a job, I answered an ad recruiting wom-
en to be Playboy Bunnies, as the Club at Great Gorge had officially opened.
Decked in a leotard and tights, I participated in a group interview after filling
in my address and measurements on a questionable application. I was inspect-
ed similar to the way Msgr. Feeley did when I tried out for cheerleading in
high school, both times failing because of substandard legs.

This time it was my thighs
too much space appeared between them
one of those blessings in disguise.

A few months later, I felt stable enough to visit my cousin, Merry, in Palmyra. Her mom appreciated me in ways my own mom never could. When I
was there, I performed every task she'd ask me to do, behaving like my sister,
a parent's dream in my cousin's home. So when Merry asked if I'd like to come
live with them, it was an easy decision to make. My sister and her husband were
contemplating a move to Panama, and the thought of living without them to
buffer the reality of our parents' relationship, fired up my anxiety to near panic
proportions.

Of course, my mom hated the idea. "Why do you want to live at Lucia's and
not stay here with me?" The thought of it crushed her, but I didn't seem to
care. I was feeling better, and I missed my cousin, Merry, my drinking buddy
and partner in crime. So I packed up my clothes, stuffed them into our blue
VW, and headed south to Palmyra, a town across the river from Philadelphia,
the two places where I'd spend my next five years.

My Aunt Lu was two years older than Mom and in her eyes, the favored
child while growing up. She was the one who did no wrong, leading to the
same type of sibling rivalry I experienced with my sister, one our mother un-
consciously passed on and set in motion. But I was the queen at Aunt Lu's
house. My Uncle Bill's favorite niece named Carol. The one who brought him

his after dinner *ain-it* (vodka in coffee) each night.

Uncle Bill's drinking was slow and steady to Aunt Lu's binging. Though he drank every night, she could go for months without having a sip. But you'd better duck when she'd go on a bender. She would transform from her usual Dr. Jekyll self into the monstrous Mrs. Hyde, with one flick of her vodka-glugging wrist. While Uncle Bill drank for all the world to see, Aunt Lu hid pints under her car seat or in closets in the house. The chief difference in their home and mine, their relationship versus my parents', was their abiding love for each other, though alcohol abuse gradually chinked away at its structure. While my father exhibited the same affection for my mother, it was not returned.

Something Mom never fully grasped
until she herself was forced to stop drinking.

I earned my keep the first few months helping around the house, but having kids still living at home was a strain on their limited budget, so I was soon forced to get a job. The thought of it overwhelmed me. I signed up with a temp agency, getting filing jobs here and there, earning enough to pitch in for food and nights out with Merry, though we rarely paid for our drinks.

My cousin worked at a law firm, with a law-school student named, Jeff, who also loved to party. On Friday nights, we'd meet at McGillin's Old Ale House on Drury Street in Philly, Jeff's favorite haunt, just around the corner from where they worked. We'd sit for hours with non-stop beer pitchers feeding our thirst, and when the bar closed down at 2:00, we'd head to Jeff's, to smoke pot with his wife, the mom to his four kids. We'd lay on their basement rug, with the harmonic tones of the Bee Gees seeping through three-foot speakers, laughing and dozing as dawn trickled in. Too wasted to care about safety, the subway and bus back to Palmyra became a familiar excursion, as did crawling into bed until late Saturday afternoon, a much needed ritual, to sleep off the previous night's escapades.

We'd heard of a doctor who doled out prescriptions for what we called Black Beauties, the meth of our day, a little black diet pill that allowed us to drink and stay up all night without dozing off. As we were always on diets, mandatory for women back then, they would serve a dual purpose. We found our way to his Northeast Philly office, squeezed into the row houses of that area, not far from my cousin's childhood home. After a brief interview about our dieting woes, we left with a script for the pills. We'd go back a number of times for refills.

The combination of black beauties and liquor

made for a great night of partying

the mainstay of our lives.

It was during my stay at my aunt's that I started seeing married men. Alcohol allowed me to do things I knew were wrong, to the point of celebrating the defiance.

My first dalliance was with my boss, Scott, who presided over the insurance company I was temping for. Scott was in his late 40s, unhappily married, or so he said. I was still incredibly naïve and feeling sorry for his situation. I let him take me to dinner, where we drank copious amounts of wine, after which we checked into hotel rooms, for nights of unsatisfying sex. The job only lasted a couple months, and so did the fling with Scott.

More than sleeping with a married man, I was actually participating in my boss's sexual harassment of me, a behavior we didn't have a term for back then, let alone a law that protected us from it.

My next married man was Kent, another fledgling lawyer, who also worked with my cousin at the firm, and often drank with us at McGillin's on Friday nights. Kent had once been in the seminary and was married to an ex-nun, and wrote scads of poetry for me in the style of e.e. cummings, the poet my sister and I treasured in college. Still seeking the love I'd longed for as a young child, I found it in Kent, who worshipped the ground I walked on for 14 months of my wayward life. I loved the intrigue of meeting in clandestine places, stealing time whenever we could, and in brief moments of soberness, arguing in my head over his marital status and strong reverence for his partner in life. I remember the first time we had sex and how quickly he came, how apologetic he was, his desire for me so overwhelming, how intoxicating and alluring that was. Ours was mostly an emotional affair, one we entertained with the constant companion of liquor, which played a key role in all relationships I had with men.

Which was about to take on a whole new meaning

when my cousin and I moved out of her house

and into our own apartment in center city Philadelphia.

That roller coaster ride of one-night stands

and accompanying blackouts was about to begin.

chapter fifteen

A Shot of Validation

My sister doesn't understand why I'm cutting her off. She's been away for so long, and now that we have a chance to renew things, why would I want to cut the cord? She's sober too, and on my side, which causes me great confusion. I talk to my therapist about this, who openly supports my pulling away. She knows the bond that co-dependents share. The one with my sister is even stronger than the tie with my mom.

Of course, my mom is still drinking, so separation from her seems easier to do. I sense it will raise her consumption even more. And though I know I'm not responsible for the amount she drinks, it's still a hard one for me to grasp.

I've tried controlling it for as long as I can remember and failed every time.

I've done the same with my husband, who has pieces of my mom and my dad woven into his personality. The way he holds a grudge is much like my mom, his gift of attentive listening, like my dad. I still long to reconcile with him, but fear we're growing in different directions. Since I've unleashed my anger, I've become increasingly aware of my fury towards him.

Your willingness to forgive his affair
in only a month's time, is a thing of the past.

I go see another movie, as I work to increase the courage to step out on my own. This time I'm certain it won't scare me half to death. I see *Thelma and*

Louise, at the same dollar theater I nearly freaked out at a few months before. I find myself rooting for these women-turned-criminals with the rest of the crowd. The audience is mostly female, in a town that's considerably gay, and we all cheer loudly when Louise pulls the trigger. Too many of us know what it's like to be in Thelma's victim-packed shoes. I leave the theater exhilarated, slightly different from the time before, fist pumping to myself the whole ride home.

> *This experience*
> *is a shot of validation*
> *for the person you are aiming to become.*

After acing the first course I take, I quickly sign up for another. This may be just the magic potion I need. Doing well in school was never my thing. Being a clown was more to my liking. Maybe it's time to trade that comic persona for something new. The idea terrifies me. Who will I be without my funny? I'm not sure I even want to find out. I know recovery is serious business, so it almost seems I have no choice.

I try it out on family and old friends, and they're not quite sure how to respond to me. My light-hearted self, which is more to their liking, seems to have vanished or been misplaced. Unsure of what to make of this new version of me, their indirect remarks reveal they miss the old model.

I go back to therapy with that husband of mine and find it hard to sit beside him on the so-called loveseat in Renée's office. She rocks in her maple chair, scribbling on yellow lined paper as we both complain. We continue to fling the *you-always* at each other, just as we did the last time we were here. We put up shields to defend ourselves from the arrows we sling. We're engaged in a competition no one can win.

> *This new-ish you*
> *who's letting go of old-ish you*
> *is confusing him as much as it is you.*

At my CoDA meeting, someone shares a copy of Melodie Beattie's *The Language of Letting Go.* It's a book of meditations written by the woman who helped put codependency on the recovery map. She talks about the simple reflections and how they've changed her life. I buy a copy and read it everyday. It becomes my bible, the words it contains help me reconfigure my own.

I learn to set boundaries with my husband, telling him he can't just hug me whenever he wants. From here on out, he needs to ask me first. He thinks I've lost my mind. "What man has to ask his wife if he can hug her?"

I tremble as I say, "You do," suspecting the ground I stand on might collapse beneath my feet. My guilt is like quick sand, ready to gobble me up. I long to apologize, to make that guilt go away. Instead I bite my tongue.

I've spent a lifetime apologizing when I shouldn't have.

Though he made a big stink, the next time I see him he asks.

I still have trouble sleeping. Fear grips me when I put the day to rest. I was hoping church might relieve some of that, but the clicking of Rusty's nails, my beloved Chocolate Lab, wakes me each time he circles for a new position. Going back to sleep seems a lost cause. After discussing this with my therapist—making decisions without her is not up for grabs—I force him to sleep downstairs, like an unfaithful husband.

The first night's rough for all of us, as my daughter's still starting out in my bed. Cries and whimpers rise from the family room, reminding us of our loss. We both end up crying, right along with our dog. Without Rusty in my room, after tucking my daughter into her own bed, the dreams I had as a kid show up in the gloom of night. The ones that paralyze my body, as I sense the presence of an intruder. When I try moving to protect myself, I can't seem to budge.

My days are filled with foggy brain and are difficult to get through.

One of my new friends from CoDA swears she can help with that, using healing modalities I've never heard of. Homeopathy is one of them. She invites me and my daughter for dinner and explains how it works. It sounds similar to the allergy shots I received as a child. Her two young kids take a liking to my daughter. While watching them play, I can't remember ever being as trusting as they are with each other.

You'll soon uncover what this lack of trust stems from.

A part of your life you've worked hard to forget.

chapter sixteen

_____

Of Wenching and Campaigning

My cousin and I rented a trinity house at 1923 Rodman, a narrow one-way street between Lombard and South, the street made famous by a song, bordering Center City and South Philly. Originally built for servants and slaves, trinity houses got their Father, Son, Holy Ghost identity from their stacked layout, and usually contained only one room per floor. We were lucky. Ours came with two on the first floor, a tiny living area and even smaller kitchen. It was our first real place together; one we could call ours and considered charming.

Merry took the second floor, next to the bathroom, as her small bladder required a close proximity to the toilet. Which gave me the third-floor bedroom, where getting a bed to this level felt almost impossible. The narrow, curved stairwell was a serpentine force to be reckoned with. After a day spent moving in and hoisting beds through windows, we met our next-door neighbors, Terry and Molly, who took us around the corner to The Graduate, a neighborhood bar where we'd soon become regulars. It was a reason to celebrate, and celebrate we did. Throwing back shots and beer with two girls who knew how to party like we did, reassured us we'd found the right place.

Terry was a law student, who worked for a new city agency called the Court Bail Program, which got defendants out on bail through Release on Recognizance (ROR). It was a fairly new venture and Terry thought I might be able to find some kind of employment with them. This jazzed me up, as I'd not felt gainfully employed since leaving college.

Finding myself, through a drunken haze, was difficult to do.

Back then, I had no clue.

I got hired as a file clerk, rectifying the boredom that job provides with lunches at McGillin's. Their Rueben sandwiches were washed down with frosty mugs of beer that would see me through long afternoons fumbling in the filing cabinets. On days too hung-over to stand the smell of brew, we'd head over to the Reading Terminal Market, where a galaxy of ethnic foods awaited our consumption.

I soon became eligible to assist law students in the interview phase of the program to assess eligibility for release. These interviews were conducted in the city prison system and Holmesburg was one they visited. I was told to wear something baggy, a sweater that concealed a good portion of my shape. We had this discussion over beers the night before my first encounter, a night I tossed and turned in my third-floor bed.

Holmesburg was built in 1896 and its massive four-foot thick fieldstone walls encircling its wheel spoke design hearkened back to medieval castles. Its guard towers that peered down on visitors were like the scowling brows of kings. Just a few years before my visits, an inmate riot raged through the cafeteria, taking 500 police officers to restore order in this dungeon of a place. I entered those massive walls with as much trepidation as a six-year-old stepping into their first haunted house, with no viable saliva to muster a decent gulp. Despite the baggy clothes, the gawks and stares of its inmates left me feeling naked, and deemed it necessary to chug enough beer to plaster me to the sweat-stained sheets of my bed that night. I wasn't sure how many times I wanted to put myself through that sort of scrutiny.

Shortly after our move into Philly, my brother-in-law accepted a job as a Panama Canal Pilot to navigate ships through the famed waterway, and re-located my sister and their family to its tropical home. My sister and I were always close, becoming even closer during my long bout of anxiety and panic attacks. She'd been my confidant and my rock, but her family had become her focus, and our lives were obviously moving in different directions. Even so, I felt a deep loss with this move, a severance of our connectedness, another abandonment that triggered my underlying pain.

I handled it the only way I knew how.

I drank more than usual.

A few months after they left, I received a letter from her, telling me how home-sick she was, crying each time she heard a patriotic tune play. She invited Merry and me to come visit for Christmas. I was ecstatic at the thought and fortunately my employment status afforded me time. They lived in inexpensive government housing on the Atlantic side of the Canal Zone, within a tight-knit community of ship pilots and their families, who were lured by this exotic lifestyle and the large salaries this position provided. They would live there for 24 years, my only sister and her family, which caused me grief for much of that time.

Merry and I fit right in with this group of expats, whose nights were spent entertaining each other. They threw large boisterous parties, forming bonds with other nostalgic souls, using alcohol to escape the ache. We were basically a part of tropic-party-central and enjoyed every minute of our time with them.

One night, while helping prepare some exotic curry dish with Capt. Calkins, a pilot who we'd take a canal transit with during our stay, we dropped the bag of basmati rice all over the kitchen floor. We were so blitzed, we quickly sank to our knees in hysterics, attempting to pick up the mess, kernel by kernel.

Our transit through the Canal was onboard a German container ship, one we boarded in the wee hours of morning, after spending the night at another Canal Zone party. Of course, we were ready to dive into a bit of the hair of the dog. It came in the form of a continuous flow of German beer, leaving us giddy as the ship crossed the 50-mile length of this celebrated passage.

During our stay, my cousin met a pilot who became smitten with her and she agreed to stay on with him. She spent another month in this tropical en-clave, as I flew back home, feeling abandoned again and deeply sorry for my-self. I'd spend longer nights with Terry and Molly at The Graduate, crying into my beer, jealous of Merry's newfound love, longing to find my own. Little did we know, it would only last a month.

Making decisions
under the influence
were not ones
that always worked out.

Merry's younger sister, Jeanette, introduced us to the bar not far from where she worked. On nights we grew tired of McGillin's, we headed over to Doc Watson's to meet Jeanette and a few of her work cronies. And after spending our night laughing and gossiping about others, with pitchers of beer fueling the talk, we'd head down to Pat's Steaks for a 2am nibble, often with guys we'd spend the rest of the night with.

One night, Jeanette, who eventually moved in with us—squeezing a bed next to the washing machine in the basement of our tiny quarters—introduced me to one of her co-workers, a gregarious and funny guy named Doug. Doug was whip smart and had a twinkle in his eye, and soon became a regular to our group, and eventually an attraction developed between us. One thing led to another and I quickly found myself sleeping with him.

Doug would drop by our apartment, empty his pockets, spilling out handfuls of drugs and amyl nitrate poppers, and we'd unwind on dalmane and beer. My first dose of amyl nitrate came in bed with Doug, who sold me on the heightened sensations the drug provides. This would be my life for the two on-and-off years we dated.

It was also the year the Flyers won the Stanley Cup, when eight of us huddled together in our tiny living room, littered with beers cans and empty pill packets, singing "God Bless America" with Kate Smith. All of us screamed in unison as they blocked a goal or smacked one in, as we drank and drugged the night away. We dedicatedly lined Broad Street to watch the Mummers who helped celebrate their win, strutting along after our nights of faithful encouragement.

We were onboard for anything that harbored an excuse
to raise our glasses and drink some more.

It was also the year of a class 4 Pap smear, my cervical dysplasia diagnosis, a precancerous condition caused by having multiple partners, a behavior directly related to my drinking. I found a surgeon who performed a cone biopsy to remove the precancerous cells. But what he couldn't remove was my increasing drive toward obliteration.

Doug lived outside the city in a rented tudor-style home with two other guys, and a woman I became fast friends with. Her name was Helene, called Chili Bean by her beau, who quickly became Chil to the rest of us. She was a woman of boundless exuberance and energy, and could talk the pants off a homeless man, making him feel grateful as he handed them over to her. She was that persuasive. Her humor knew no bounds and could turn anything you uttered into a snappy pun. When we were with Helene, our cheeks ached at the end of the night. A loving and generous soul, she took a fancy to Merry and me and injected more fun into our lives.

Helene was one of us, a kindred spirit, who smoked lots of pot, and loved to party and drink. She was an entertainer at heart and could sing all the songs from any show you named, choreographing the dances as she sang. She'd set up a full-length mirror to dance in front of, practicing moves she would use for the auditions she'd attend. She drew me into her world of musical theater, hearkening back to my high school musical days. I felt the comfort of that exhilarating world settling in. She took it seriously, and ended up quitting her financially secure job as secretary in some bigwig law firm, to take a shot at show biz. She believed strongly that life should be fun and has been doing it ever since.

She took me to my first audition, for a part in a play I can't recall, following her tryout that I watched from the wings. I was excruciatingly bad, nerves getting the best of me, but felt accomplished for even trying. A month or so later, she saw an ad for a children's repertory theatre company seeking actors. We auditioned together and got the gig.

I quit my job at ROR and hit the road with Helene and the rest of the cast, Bobby, Emit, and Earl, whom we lived with and put up with for the next year or so. I was Pinocchio to Helene's Blue Fairy, Owl to her Piglet, Paula Revere to her Betsy Ross. We did the school circuit, pulling our Dream Makers van into school parking lots, dragging sets onto grade school stages, and performed for audiences of excited kids. We spent nights in shoddy motel rooms, drinking cheap red wine and munching on cheese doodles. For a while it was fun. After traveling all day, setting up and striking sets, we grew weary of it all and looked for other work.

Around this time, Merry's dad, my dear Uncle Bill, found blood in his stool and was diagnosed with colon cancer. A daily drinker for all the years I knew him, his love affair with liquor was catching up, a link no one wanted to make. He ended up spending weeks at Jefferson Hospital, where Merry, Jeanette, and I took turns sitting with him, holding his hand, watching this man of considerable girth and personality, shrink away to a mere 90 pounds. He died less than a year after his diagnosis, the first of our parents to go, and we made sure to usher him out the way our family knew best.

We all got bombed.

I remember the send-off in their Palmyra home, where I'd spent many nights at the dining room table, taking in my uncle's liberal politics. They were an oppositional view to my father's, a die-hard Republican who once slapped me for saying something hostile about Richard Nixon. On the day of my uncle's funeral, I stood perched on those stairs, reciting the soliloquy from Hamlet, remembering every word, one my uncle had recited hundreds of times: "To be or not to be, that is the question...."

An apt farewell to a beloved man.

I sobbed for an hour after taking a bow.

I ended that night in a motel room with one of my cousin Rob's dear friends, a guy they called Red, one of his many friends I crushed on in high school. We spent the night having grief sex the day we said good-bye to my uncle.

For the next two years, my Aunt Lu would fall into a cycle of binging, dealing with her husband's death the way many do, slipping into the sweet oblivion of alcohol.

The next audition Helene whisked me off to was at the Warwick Hotel, for a 16th century dinner theatre that was opening there. They were looking for wenches, a far cry from the children's theater we'd been doing. Though I sensed I'd fit right into its bawdy atmosphere, with the rowdy experiences I'd been having the last six years or so. We both got hired and quickly became known as Wench Lulu and Wench Lilly.

Touted as "an X-rated restaurant, recommended for all those willing to let themselves go," it was somewhat modest by today's standards. We'd greet sedate customers as they streamed through the doors, loosening ties and throwing arms around blushing men who accompanied wives or girlfriends somewhat miffed, then sling pitchers of beer and carafes of wine as we sang songs chosen for the atmosphere. Front and center, a portly Henry VIII ruled the stage, eyeing and pinching wenches, as did the increasingly inebriated theater-goers. At the time, it was a fun way to make money, as generous tips slipped into cleavages while the night wore on.

A few months into the gig, the manager of the theater said the chain was doing so well, they'd be opening another in Albany and Atlantic City. Helene and I volunteered to help train the wenches. We spent two weeks in each location. I lost my voice in Atlantic City, from nods that developed with all the yelling the job required, and met a guy who, aside from pleasuring myself, gave me my first genuine orgasm, his unselfish love making a novelty to me.

One night, after returning to the Philadelphia theater, a well-dressed group of outsiders came in for a show. We discovered they worked for the Carter campaign, whose Pennsylvania headquarters was situated on the fourth floor of the hotel. With them was a handsome state senator, who was managing the Pennsylvania campaign. He had swoon-worthy looks and a roving eye that immediately grabbed my attention.

The following week, I found myself at their headquarters, signing up as a volunteer, and climbing aboard for the last big push of the campaign, for a presidential candidate I knew little about. I spent my days on the phone bank, pouring through numbers of registered Dems, making sure they turned out to vote. My nights were spent wenching, then meeting up with campaign staffers for brews at the Warwick's bar. They became campaign cronies, this group of young Irishman from Boston, all previous campaigners, and all hoping to elect this man and receive an administration job in exchange. They believed in Carter the same way Josh and Sam believed in Bartlett. The atmosphere was heady and pulled me into its ride.

My first real encounter with the senator was at one of our end-of-day soirees, this one held at Jack Sullivan's home in Jenkintown, a suburb of Philly. Jack had graduated from Annapolis with Carter, and though he was a registered Republican, he was his right-hand man in Pennsylvania. Booze was as prominent a fixture at these gatherings as was campaign talk. These people worked their butts off, pulling 18-hour days, 7 days/week, the rule of thumb for this type of work. A novice campaigner, I was incredibly intimidated by this well-informed gaggle of professionals, which of course, led me to drink that much more.

How I ended up in a conversation with the senator is beyond me, but attraction drew me into such exchanges. Back in the day, I was fluent at flirting, laying on charms like thickly spread caviar, too hard to resist this sought-after delicacy.

And always behind it was a desperate need for love.

The love I felt gypped of as a young child.

He drove a carload of us back to the city, with the intention of dropping us off. Instead, as I sat beside him in the front seat of his campaign-provided towncar, he invited me back to his digs, the Windsor Suites on Ben Franklin Parkway, for a nightcap, a signal something more would happen on this notorious night. That would be the first of many nights I'd spend with him, sneaking out in early morning so no one would see. His prestige became a drug. Gaining status by having sex with a politician was a thrill-seeking thing to do. It brought me into the inner circle, and I was soon asked to take over the elder vote. I was taken off the phone banks, and given an office of my own, climbing the ladder for a candidate that was still a foreigner to me.

It made me feel important, accomplished in a way I'd never felt before, moving up the ranks of life, gaining status, always looking outside myself for some sense of significance. The day I accompanied the advance team for Carter's presidential debate at the Walnut Theater, put me on the top rung, looking down. I had arrived, or so it seemed.

The advance team was laden with Secret Service and my wisecracking ways did little to impress this group of stony-faced men. Afterwards, I remember drinking myself into oblivion, then heading over to the senator's apartment, for uninvited sex. It was not the only time I'd do this. The last instance, I found out about his wife and kids, who were coming for the last week before the election. He sent me away, humiliation dripping off me like greasy slime, the shame keeping my eyes averted for days. I watched election results in a haze of booze, celebrating our peanut farmer from Georgia, whom we helped get into the White House.

Of course, the highlight of working on a presidential campaign at this level is the Inaugural invitation I received, for parties and all. I could bring two friends, so my two cousins accompanied me on this historic trip. I bought a full-length black gown, splotched with big red rose blossoms, something that would make me stand out from the crowd. Attention seeking had become a full-time job. I drank excessively at the ball we attended, having little memory of the president and Rosalyn coming in for the traditional crowd-pleasing dance, too smashed to genuinely enjoy the moment.

Shortly after the election, we moved from our cozy Rodman Street apartment to a sprawling eight-bedroom home on the west side of the Schuylkill, in the 4200 block of Walnut Street that Terry's cousin, Dan, was renting with some U-Penn students. Terry had moved in a few months before and persuaded us to join her in this lower-rent venture.

This move would be the continuation of my undoing.

My life unraveling before me

one venomous drink at a time.

chapter seventeen

Lost, But Finding Your Way

I start writing poetry, some primitive verse that fourth graders might scrawl. It helps me make sense of things, while searching for the self I once was. Before alcohol mangled every intrinsic part of me. I long to become more solid for my daughter, who often seems as lost as me.

We wade through the swamp of change

hoping to step out leech free.

She has three little friends living close by that often fill in when I'm at odds with myself. Most days tip in that direction. The twins she's grown up with play dress-up at our house, twirling in skirts I once loved wearing, clomping in heels, playing girls with my precious daughter. I sense they may be gay long before they become aware of it themselves. The girl down the street, who dined at our Christmas table, is my daughter's first girl crush. She's a fixture in our home and an older sister of sorts. Her military parents work different shifts at the local Air Force base. Her dad often stops by when he's had a few too many. I don't know this now, though his dark side is fairly evident, that he will tumble from a tree, with a six-pack by his side, leaving his children fatherless, and way more lost than my own. I tell him about being sober, how sobriety has changed my life. I try nonchalantly to persuade him to do the same. But he clings to his disease like that husband of mine. He guards steadfastly with all the might he can muster, refusing to give up one of the loves of his life.

You remember the feeling.
You did it for years.

Though I often feel helpless, as yearning to be rescued is hardwired to my brain, repairing things myself feeds my starving self-assurance. Memories of spark-plug and oil changes still bubble in my heart. When something stumps my do-it-myself-ness, I struggle with asking for help. It's a pattern I developed as a young child with a hospitalized mom, who wasn't there to do things when I needed her to. It seems that men like rescuing vulnerable women, as those fairy tales I stopped reading to my daughter used to say. They sniff out trouble before a smoke signal even goes up.

My loneliness accepts help from these men, from one who'll end up molesting his own daughter. A dark spot in my past seems to seek these people out, as I haven't yet touched on this tenuous topic in therapy. It's boiling to the surface, ready to spew. But I hold it back as my therapist advises, thinking I'm not yet strong enough to deal with the unsightly brew.

My therapy sessions with my husband seem stalled. We recycle our issues like the bottles and cans I take out with the trash. I notice something different in the way he behaves, wearing his indifference like a t-shirt that needs to be tossed. The familiarity of this behavior is nauseatingly real. As we sit on the love seat, in her well-lit office, light streaming through windows that encircle the room, I ask if he's been seeing other women. His hesitation is louder than any words he finally says. Our therapist stares him down, wheedling out an answer, sooner than he'd like to supply. He goes on about his need for sex, a spiel I've heard many times before. "After all, we're separated. What do you expect me to do?"

I leave the session crestfallen, holding back tears till I'm locked safely inside my car. Through no fault of her own, my daughter spilled this same can of beans the week before, another knife blade to my grief-stricken heart. I chose not to believe her. Now I have no choice. The question becomes, what will I do with this information? I'll steam about it all the way home, trying hard not to take it out on my daughter when I finally see her.

I know I'm not ready to let go of him yet. I need to hold on to some semblance of hope, some particle of chance that we can work things out. I am so enmeshed with the illusion I can have a healthy relationship with this man, I can't think straight.

You tell him he needs to stop drinking.
You tell him not to call you for a week.
You end up calling him before week's end.
He is another addiction of yours.
One you can't seem to quit.

The oldest daughter of our neighbor across the street is getting married. Much to my surprise, my husband has been experimenting with not drinking. It's been almost a month. This will be a major part of the experiment. Being around people drinking is a hard thing to do. I feel a little wobbly myself.

We sit at a table with our neighbor down the street. She's in her 80s and lost her husband a few years back. She's vivacious and funny, and always talks to me as I walk by her yard with my dog. Her matter-of-fact manner is often the highlight of my day. My husband asks her to dance, a sweet gesture that hasn't gone unnoticed. And as the wedding reception draws to a close, she gives him a kiss on the lips, a kiss he'll talk about for years to come.

He laughs, with his twinkling Irish blue eyes. The ones I fell in love with when we first met. I leave thinking we may still have a chance to make things work. He even talks about what it was like for him not drinking. Not as bad as he thought. Little do I know, this experiment of his won't last much longer.

The grip of alcohol is too tight to relinquish.

The school thing is growing on me and I decide to matriculate as a grad student. I'll take the courses I need to get my master's degree, two this semester and two the next. This will help me become as smart as my sister, a competition she has no idea she's entered. If I get my master's, I'll surely win the race. The notion of that makes me high. I quickly scold myself for having such a feeling. I haven't fully learned that it's okay to feel this way.

That it's okay to feel, period.

One of these courses is Reading K–6. We're given the choice of a final project, one that includes writing a picture book. I dream the story idea that very same night. I'll write about a princess. One who will not eat her vegetables. It will mimic my life with my daughter. I've tried different things with her, like mixing chopped kale into her mac and cheese. She hates me when I do this. And though I can't stand it when she's mad at me, I do it anyway. We go to the library and bring home a stack of picture books, more than we usually check out. I read these books with her, paying close attention to how the words and pictures lay on the page.

I work on the project every night and can't believe how much fun this is. The text is done in two weeks. I title it *The Story of Princess Margaret: A Veggie Tale*. I buy special paper to use for illustrations and enlist my daughter for that part of the project. She and the friend she adores help with the drawings. They are so precious, these girls and their illustrations. I watch my daughter compare her artwork to her friend's, thinking hers don't match up. It breaks my heart, knowing that feeling so well.

You've done that all your life.

The reason you chose to have only one child.

The child who you pray, will never pick up a drink.

chapter eighteen

_____

From Sally Bowles to DUI

When we moved into the Walnut Street house, Merry and I took bedrooms beside each other on the third floor, down the hall from Christian, a beautiful, gay man who kept us in stitches with his exuberance and wit. He was a waiter at La Terrasse, a stylish French restaurant on Sansom, not far from where we lived. He'd come strutting into our rooms without knocking, wondering how he looked before hitting the clubs after his shift was through. We adored that man, and more than once, I tried to convert him, sneaking into his room at night and slipping into his bed.

Jeanette and Terry shared the second floor with Terry's cousin, Dan, while Marilyn, Dave, and Metta, slept above us all, on the fourth floor. The house was monstrous and dark, with an Addam's Family feel to it. Dan, the soon-to-be architect, would swoon over its design, its magnificent moldings and trimmings a sight to behold.

It was an imposing Victorian-style row house we called Walnutshire.

We shared kitchen duties at night, each of us taking turns cooking and cleaning up. We also shared a wall with Grace next door, an older woman with a low tolerance for any sound at all. Our dinners were always animated, bottles of wine littering the table, voices and laughter at high pitch. Our pots and pans hung on the wall we shared with Grace, and every time someone hung a dried pot on its hook, Grace would scream from the other side, the noise from the night finally getting too much for her sensitive ears. We were too young to care enough for Grace's afflictions, often laughing when she'd scream, swearing we'd become more considerate, with efforts to change our boisterous ways only lasting a day or two.

Persuaded by my housemates who extolled my cooking abilities to get a job in a restaurant kitchen, I found an ad for an entry-level position at a fairly new restaurant on 16th and Locust called Frög. Owned by Steve Poses, an instigator of Philly's restaurant renaissance, Frög was a fusion of Asian and European cuisines, served in a cozy dining room of white linen cloths covering its forest-green tabletops. I could work the day shift again, chopping veggies in the basement prep kitchen next to Linda the baker, whose job I'd take over for a summer she was away. Eventually, I worked my way upstairs to the real kitchen. The best feature of the job was I had nights free to carouse with my housemates, and carouse we did.

We often started at Strolli's, an inexpensive Italian restaurant in South Philly, with red and white checkered tablecloths, and an owner who greeted everyone who entered his restaurant, playing his mandolin table-side during the night. Countless bottles of Chianti accompanied plates of pasta, though nothing could top Mama Strolli's Veal Piccata. We frequently stumbled out of Strolli's, moving on to another venue, as the night felt young and called out our names.

We became regulars at Smokey Joe's Tavern, a hangout for Penn students. Rubbing elbows with those smart kids gave me a feeling of worth. I had a crush on Mitchell, a bartender there, and after sleeping with him a number of times, always on a quest for true love, he eventually revealed I was not the type of girl he would settle down with. The kind who hung out at bars, getting sloppy drunk, picking up whoever would take her home on any given night.

It hurt to hear, but didn't stop my wayward lifestyle.

When bars closed at 2am, we'd find after-hour clubs to hit. Christian got out of work late and was always up for partying at that time of night. I'd go to the gay clubs with him, too drunk to know what I was doing, and cut into a pair of gorgeous guys dancing, and try to win them over to the straight side of town.

I was still seeing Doug, and regularly went out to their Main Line home for weekends of drinking and drugs. The first time I snorted cocaine was at a party they'd thrown, with a bottle full of pharmaceutical grade stash that someone had scored, and the expanse of love I felt for everyone there, even those I'm sure I disliked, was astounding. I chatted with folks I'd never have the nerve to approach, as that shy, insecure girl still resided inside me, and without booze, dictated my moves. Though I'd do coke numerous times after, it was the only time I'd ever experience such openness.

Until I got sober.

Shy or not, I recall hitchhiking to Doug's house one weekend, 25 miles away, after too much to drink at Smokey Joe's, sticking out my thumb in the heart of West Philly. With unbelievable fortune, I got rides from those who feared for my safety, arriving at his house without being abducted or raped, ringing his doorbell at 2am, blurry-eyed and desperate. I considered myself a daredevil, took pride in my risk-taking ways, doing things others never dared to do.

The increasing insanity that alcohol abuse brings.

My group of friends liked to dance and we'd often go to Greek restaurants that had bouzouki music, where we drank shots of ouzo throughout the night, circle dancing with men who longed to bed us down.

We frequently went to Penn parties, and one I distinctly remember was a night I spoke in my practiced British accent, something I'd often do, depending on my mood and how much I had to drink. I met a man named Ibrahim, a grad student from Libya, who'd been educated in London and spoke with the same accent I had that night, a man I'd have a frenzied relationship with for my remaining time in Philly. He was a Ph.D. candidate, struggling with his research for his dissertation, and was enthralled by this faux English woman, who had flirted with him and his swarthy good looks at the party that night. Though it wasn't allowed in his native country, Ibrahim liked to drink, and we soon became entangled by our common interests.

Sex and booze.

Ibrahim was exotic and worldly, from a country I knew little about. We'd often have dinner with his Arabic friends, who spoke to each other in their native language, eating unusual foods that brought comfort to them, as I sloshed down goblets of wine to hide my own unease. They would talk about the Israeli-Palestinian situation, one they had strong feelings about, educating me from a totally different perspective. Ibrahim believed that Palestinians should do whatever it takes to reclaim land that was rightfully theirs. He supported terrorism, no matter the cost. I listened to him wide-eyed, naïve to most political situations outside our country, in awe of the passion he had for the cause, and never fully understanding the magnitude of what he believed.

Though he spoke mostly English when we were alone, he slid into Arabic when he was annoyed, which happened a lot while we were dating. He was attracted to my carefree attitude, but torn by the fact it was fueled by my drinking. I'd show up at his door at 2am, after a night out with my friends, knowing he'd been at the library much of that time, eager for a romp in the hay. This consisted of a narrow single bed in his tiny room, in some mundane grad dorm at Penn.

Sex with Ibrahim was like nothing I'd ever had before. He was patient and passionate, always considerate of my needs, always knowing what to do to bring me pleasure. He was the only man I'd ever consistently have simultaneous orgasms with. Though his passion also had a darker side. I remember him slapping me across the face for showing up at his door drunk.

Which I did quite often
prompted by my pickled brain
carrying the shame of what I was
around with me daily.

My interest in theater hadn't waned, and one summer while living in our Walnut Street commune, I attended a play in an outdoor venue near Society Hill. One of the actors had been hired to direct the Penn Players production of *Cabaret*, and was looking for his offbeat notion of Sally Bowles. Mark had spotted me in the audience, my blond hair a feature he desired, and sent someone to fetch me when the performance was over. He invited me to try out for the part, which I willingly agreed to do. I auditioned for a role I intimately identified with and knew I was meant to play. And so did Mark, as he quickly cast me as Sally, much to the disgruntlement of the remaining cast, all students at the university.

I drank after rehearsals, attempting to blot out the gripping fear that followed me as I prepared for this role, often alone in a bar not far from the Annenberg Center, pondering my part and upset about not getting things right. I dreamed of making it big, an illusion fueled by the booze.

I remember the night I sat next to Milo O'Shea at the bar, his bushy black eyebrows unforgettable to me, drinking by himself, following a rehearsal of his own. He was due to appear on the main stage with Jason Robards and Geraldine Fitzgerald, whom I'd pass in back stage hallways, in a production of O'Neill's *A Touch of the Poet*, prior to its opening on Broadway the following month. He seemed sad, and somewhat bitter about his aging, resentful of the young crop of actors who wanted fame too quickly, unwilling to do what it takes to earn their dues. We sat together for hours, sulking into our brews, and I felt mighty fortunate to receive advice from this acclaimed Irish actor. He fed me direction that would spark my performance, told me to be myself, don't try to imitate Liza Minelli, words I'd take with me to my next rehearsal, certain that some of his actorly wisdom rubbed off on me that night.

A few weeks before our opening at the Harold Prince Theater in the Annenberg Center of the Performing Arts, I'd have a not-by-chance meeting with Hal Prince, who was in the city for a performance. Helene, who always had her finger on the pulse of all things related to theater, had discovered he'd be in town. We headed over to the show, whose name eludes me, and after the final curtain, made our way backstage, informed that he was stopping by to congratulate the cast. With a gentle shove by my friend, I stuck out a clammy hand and introduced myself, telling him I'd be playing Sally Bowles at his alma mater, squeaking out, "Is there any chance you could make it to a performance?"

He was animated and kind, and said, "Send me the dates and I'll see what I can do." And as requested, I wrote a letter to remind him of the running, just a week before our opening, and received a response a week later, apologizing that he'd be in London during our run. I carried that letter in my purse for years, and would pull it out at some bar I was in, to pass around.

Always seeking attention and status.

A sad way to live a life.

During my stay at the Walnut Street house, Steve Poses, owner of Frög, had opened another restaurant called The Commissary, a gourmet cafeteria that took off like gangbusters. He also started a catering business, still going strong today that used specialties from both restaurants as its basis. The man who managed Frög was a dear friend. He had the same sense of humor as me and liked to drink. We frequently went out after a night of catering, and thought nothing of ordering a bottle of champagne to start us off.

By this time, I'd managed to work my way into the kitchen, to the salad station, my new assignment and a madhouse at lunch service. I worked in this cramped space with a man named Paul Roller, our luncheon chef and a tough boss, whom I frequently quibbled with, as two strong personalities in the kitchen could stir up a lot of heat. One day, after a night of heavy drinking, I was attempting to open a vinegar bottle, battering the top of it with a large chef's knife. I was angry about something Paul said, who was pressuring me to get my station set, and just like that, the knife slipped and sliced open my hand. Upon seeing what happened, Paul grabbed a clean kitchen towel. He ran around his station to assess my injury and winced as he looked.

"How bad is it?" I asked in a wobbly voice. I was already feeling faint.

"Not bad at all," slid from Paul's mouth, as he quickly wrapped the towel around my hand, calculating what to do next.

After ordering his sous-chef to take over lunch service, he whisked me out the back door, ran me down Locust Street, holding my hand together with the now bloody kitchen towel, over 20th Street to Graduate Hospital. I was rushed into surgery by Dr. Kaplan, a McDreamy of a man, who used 132 stitches, with the aid of a microscope, to close up the wound. Paul and I were forever bonded by the experience; this man, who probably saved my hand, will always hold a chunk of my heart.

We also hung out with a group of guys that stage-crewed at the Annenberg, who built sets and designed lighting for their notable productions. The crew as we called them, consisted of three highly entertaining men. Godfrey, a small-framed man who walked with a limp, wobbling his head as he spoke and characteristic of his native India, had fascinating stories of his homeland that he loved to tell. Dave, who spoke with a slight southern drawl, was a tall surfer-looking blonde, the quiet one with piercing blue eyes, whom I seriously crushed on any time he came into view. And then there was Chic (Jude Ciccolella), an aspiring actor, who spoke in a low growl, and kept us all in stitches. He'd eventually move on to having a steady stage and screen career as a character actor, cast in such movies as *The Shawshank Redemption, Sin City,* and *The Terminal.*

We'd intentionally run into them, as their theater stories filled us with delight, building sets on Broadway when the Annenberg season closed, and going into elaborate details about their construction. We'd drink with them well into the night, and often go home with one or the other afterwards.

I also started running while living in Philly, a good way to sweat off the beer I drank the night before. I discovered I could eat and drink as much as I wanted without gaining weight and became a diehard runner for many years.

It fooled me into feeling healthy

while keeping my denial solidly intact.

It was during this time that Terry was experimenting with her sexuality, trying on girls to see how they fit. After a day of drinking at the bacchanalian feast her mom threw every year near her Swarthmore home, we ended up back in Terry's room, with me as one of her experiments. We never got further than luscious kissing, and though I was drunk enough to fully enjoy the experience, I slammed on the brakes before it could accelerate. I sensed it was not the thing I wanted to add to and further confuse my already chaotic life.

At some point, I felt the need to see a therapist. My level of anxiety about my life was ever increasing, and in equally strong denial of its cause. Dr. Puhalla would be my second stab at achieving a semblance of peace and might provide the cure. I complained to him about the mounting pressure I felt to find a partner and raise a white-picket-fence sort of family.

When he asked me, "How much do you drink?" I lied about the amount, like most problem drinkers do.

"Oh, maybe three or four drinks a night," I said, and even with my substantial lie, he thought I drank too much.

He said, "Heavy drinkers not only quash their feelings with the alcohol they consume, but the hangovers serve the same purpose. They live in a haze of repression from morning to night."

He recommended I stop drinking altogether.

I never went back to see him.

Things would get much worse because of it.

I was taking on more catering gigs with my friend, Ron, becoming closer and closer to this gay man whom I honestly adored. He was also educated as a teacher, who had taught high school for a number of years. We laughed about our slide from that honorable profession, over bottles of wine and snifters of Grand Marnier, going to clubs where we wouldn't be seen by his burly boyfriend.

One night, after far too much to drink, he took me home to his beautifully appointed house in Chestnut Hill. I ended up in bed with him, and during this particular romp in the sack, he literally fell out of bed, onto his impeccably kept hardwood floor, which caused a roar of laughter to erupt in the dark. We'd sleep together a few more times, under the same veil of intoxication, before I left Philadelphia.

One of those times, with considerable consequence.

After witnessing the success of the John Bloom's 1520AD franchise, Helene and her boyfriend decided to open a similar venue outside the city in King of Prussia, calling it O'Henry! Olde British Theatre, and implored me to take part in their new adventure.

One night, after finding out that Doug was not only seeing another woman, but was seriously considering marrying her, I got so blitzed I was bleary-eyed, and unfit to operate an automobile. My friends wanted to drive me home. "But what will I do with my car?" was my misplaced main concern. I insisted on driving, and weaved from lane to lane on the almost vacant Schuylkill Expressway, closing one eye to see me through, finally getting stopped by a trooper at 3:00 in the morning. After performing a breathalyzer test that I undoubtedly failed, I was arrested for DUI, amazingly my first, and was taken to the precinct to sober up. My housemate, Terry, rescued me and posted bail, bringing me back the next day for my hearing and car retrieval.

I was sentenced to the Safe Driving Clinic, sponsored by The Main Line Council on Alcoholism and Other Drug Use. Though I fit right into the Council's description, I was far from ready to embrace my disorder. I attended all four weekly sessions, watching scenes of gruesome accidents caused by drunk driving, paid my $25 fee, but was nowhere near owning up to my increasingly debilitating condition.

My heart knew something was wrong
but my denial kept that knowledge at bay.

I was also growing a bit uneasy with my new relationship with Helene. Although she was still a wench, she was also my boss, causing an underlying current of resentment, and one I hid even from myself. Problem drinkers play this game well, hiding their true feelings that over time get expressed in some passive-aggressive way.

One Saturday, when I was scheduled to work at O'Henry!, I went to a daytime wedding, and after drinking an ample amount of champagne, I tottered into work. Dan, our manager, was not happy with my inebriated state. I quarreled with him, citing what I thought was a more than logical argument. "What difference does it make? I'm a wench. I'll fit right in."

He fired me.

My days of professional wenching were over
but my drinking continued to march on
dragging my wretch of a life with it.

The following spring, Terry announced she was moving to South Carolina. And Merry, my dear cousin and partner of sorts for the last ten years, was going with her. I was stricken with grief by this announcement. What would I do without Merry in my everyday life? The thought provoked the same sense of desertion I felt when my sister moved to Panama.

A pattern that would repeat itself
with some regularity
throughout my life.

I knew I couldn't stay in our house. The grief I felt living with them on a daily basis eventually broke through my haze of booze and hangovers. I'd find a place of my own, something I'd never done before, an adventure of epic proportions for someone who had never before lived alone in her life.

A move that would only last six months.

My parents met one night over a bridge table, a card game they both loved to play. They had a stormy relationship, but stayed together until my dad died, less than a year after my daughter was born.

That's me on the left, in my OLV high school uniform, with my brothers, Phil and John, in the middle, and my sister, Sui, on the right. We obviously weren't thrilled about this photoshoot.

Thanksgiving was held at my Aunt Lu's that year, when my grandpa was living with them. In the front row are my cousins, Rob and Liz, and their cousin, Lenny, with my sister, Grandpa, me, and my cousin, Merry, in the back row. I had this photo in my wallet for years.

Here I am with my youngest brother, Phil, the two rebels of the family. That dress I have on is the skirt I bought in Saint-Rémy-de-Provence, on my trip to Europe with Rickey.

My brother, John, and his wife Kathy, got married right out of college, and are still together today. My brothers share my love of baseball, though they're fans of the "other" NY team.

My sister and her husband, Phil, outside their Panama home, where they moved when my brother-in-law became a ship pilot on the Panama Canal. They lived there for 24 years. I missed her muchly.

*My favorite uncle named Bill
and Aunt Lucia, who welcomed me
to live in their home.*

*Paul, the oldest of my six cousins,
got sober a few years before me
and was hugely supportive when I
did the same.*

*My cousins: Merry, Jeanette, Liz, and Steve,
all smiles on the back porch of the
Palmyra home I moved into.*

*Ed, the son of my uncle Bill's twin
brother, Frank, was one of the
funniest guys I've ever known.
My daughter says she wouldn't
be here if he hadn't introduced
me to her dad.*

All decked out in my waitress uniform, standing in front of The Breakers in Palm Beach, where Merry and I worked one winter.

The lake house, where the 'infamous' party took place, where my sister met her husband, and sadly, where my dad died.

I met JoAnn (on the right) on the first day of college and we hit it off right away. She had the same sense of humor as me and we did some wacky things that kept us in stitches.

My cousin, Merry, who's just six days older than me, putting up with her drama queen cousin.

Here we are sitting on the stoop of our Rodman St. apartment in Philly, happy to finally have our own place.

My friend, Helene, as the Blue Fairy, scolds me in our Dream Makers' production of Pinocchio, while Earl and Bobby scheme beside us.

Here I'm singing "Don't Tell Mama," as Sally Bowles, a part I was made for, in a production of Cabaret at the Harold Prince Theater in The Annenberg Center at UPenn.

A rollicking group of performers pose at "Oh Henry! Olde British Theatre." I'm on top left as Wench Lulu, and Helene, Wench Lily, is in the center extending her leg.

My invitation to Jimmy Carter's Inauguration and inaugural ball.

On the left, Rickey takes in the beautiful view at Slea Head on the Dingle Peninsula in Ireland, a place he fit right in. The above photo is of me and our Citroën 2CV rental, when we reached Col de I'Iseran, the highest paved pass in the Alps, on our way to Italy. We were forced to turn around due to unplowed snow-filled roads in the month of June.

I played the part of Nellie Forbush in a community production of South Pacific *when I moved to Massachusetts. Here I'm singing, "I'm Gonna Wash That Man Right Outta My Hair," which I did on stage every night.*

My favorite baby picture of Maggie,
my one and only child, who's been
through a lot with me.

Her dad graduated from SU and
of course, Mag was in charge of
letting everyone know.

A tender photo of my mom and dad,
visiting Maggie together, for the first time.

My dear sister, Sui, beside my
garden, as Maggie pets our
kitty, Nellie, the first word
she said.

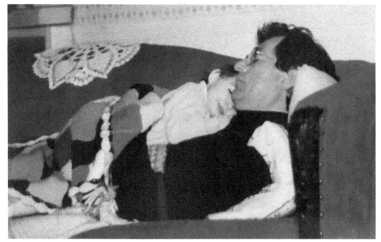

*Maggie,
taking a nap
with her daddy,
something they
loved to do.*

*Halloween, the year the Mets beat the
Sox in the World Series. This die-hard
fan dressed as Ray Knight, who was
named MVP of the series, and went
trick-or-treating with this little bunny
and her dad, who dressed as a
Red Sox player.*

*Cuddling with Maggie
on the sofa, and
sneaking a peek
at the photographer.*

Maggie with her childhood friends, Brien and Waren. It looks like "drama queen" runs in the family.

Many nights after dinner, we played a game called "Wrestling from Chicago," where Rickey and Mag sat in opposite corners of the kitchen waiting for me to bang the wooden spoon on the metal bowl to begin the match.

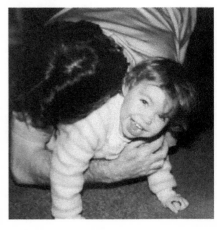

Maggie and Rusty, sharing her pillow, on a lazy Saturday afternoon.

My friendship with Trina, whom I met at one of my 12 Step meetings, made my weekends without Maggie a lot less lonely.

Mag and I spent countless hours with my friend, Sue, (back row, right) and her kids, Lizzie and Nicky. Sue introduced me to alternative ways of healing.

My friend, Burle, inspired me to become a strong, independent woman.

My writing group: Tom, Linda, Nancy, and Elaine, celebrating at my house, after my picture book was published. They made me laugh and helped me become a fairly decent writer.

A year after Maggie's dad left, we celebrated Mother's Day with him, and had some fun among the tulips in a place called Grandmother's Garden.

Here I am, looking on while Maggie plays with her cousins, at our first reunion after I stopped drinking. A gathering I was nervous about attending.

The Weis clan: Phil, me, Sui, & John, all grown up (well sort of), enjoying some winter beach time in Lavallette, the town of our younger years, while visiting our mom in NJ.

Graduation Day for my Master's Degree.
My heart was filled with gratitude and pride.

chapter nineteen

Ever Again

I discover my daughter has learned the facts of life. She's only seven when this profound experience occurs. My husband has taken over this duty I thought was mine. One my mother never shared with either me or my sister. Instead, I found out from my cousin when I was nine. An image that grossed me out for a long time. My anger and grief about losing this right of passage with my only child becomes just another sticker in my already thorny side.

Sex is a tough thing for me to think about. It was my husband's last straw, and one I have no interest in sharing with anyone but myself. I occasionally flirt with guys at AA meetings, with no intention of going anywhere with it.

A seductive habit that lingers from my drinking years.

And then the day comes in joint counseling, when it seems our therapist might be at her wits end with both of us. She suggests we go on an overnight date, away for a night without our daughter. Which means sleeping in the same bed, the two of us, with no one else around.

It's not that we haven't tried a version of this before. I've slept overnight at his apartment, with ground rules about how this would go. If he makes advances I feel I'm not ready for, he has to respect what I say. We're more like brother and sister right now, laying next to each other in our parents' double bed.

His attempts at intimacy are always turned down.

His frustration with me, a more than obvious concern.

He books a room for us near Saratoga Springs. He's excited with the prospect, while I'm wary at best. I've never had sex without the help of alcohol, and the idea causes terror and a desire to drink. But I agree to this experiment and find a baby sitter who will sleep at our house. My daughter is anxious about my leaving for the night, tugging at my already circumspect sleeve. I sense she's probably absorbed my fear.

He's agreed not to drink, so the playing field is even, and we check into our room like virginal newlyweds might do. We have a nice dinner at a local restaurant, where I sip soda water, while he has a coke. We stumble over words, both knowing what's in store, the reason we've come here: a marriage is at stake. We talk about our daughter, who we both adore. She's the incentive for trying and why my hope is still alive. I feel myself pause as he says, "I just can't imagine never being able to share another bottle of champagne with you."

The sadness in his voice is palpable
you take a sip of it
and swish it around in your head
surely a red flag of what's to unfurl.

We go back to our room, not really knowing what to do. I'm so unsure of how to start this dance, my heart's thumping a beat I can't possibly follow. He tells me to unfasten his buttons, an easier thing to do when I've had a few drinks. I possess the awkwardness of a 15-year-old with her first love and the agility of a 5-year-old learning to tie her shoelaces. I want this to be so special I can taste it on the buds of my tongue, and feel it in the tingle of my ribs. But when I slide into this hotel room bed, a clandestine act that used to insight great passion, and begin making what used to be called love with my husband, or something I thought was love, I sense the gig is up.

Though nothing is actually said
you know deep down inside
the love you're desperate to retrieve
is nowhere to be found.

Our drive home is mostly quiet, intermittently small talking each other as we speed along. Almost like neighbors who stop while I'm gardening to say hello. We gravitate towards our easy chatter, speaking of our daughter, won-

dering how she's doing. The awkwardness in this drive slouches in the backseat, itching to be home in jammies and a comfy robe.

When we see our therapist again, our sexual experiment is difficult to dis-
cuss. I know she sees it in our faces, the walls with the writing clearly written
on them. I'm still not sure how this will play out. The following month, I start
individual therapy with her, without my husband.

Soon to uncover
stuff that needs to come out
which also terrifies me.

My first day in solo therapy, I talk about my mother's hospitalization. How
I was shuffled around for a year and a half, spending three weeks here, six
months there, and a year where the worst of the stuff happened. I tell her how
I cried for three weeks straight, curled up on my cousin's bed at my mom's sister's tiny barrack home in northeast Philadelphia. It was the logical place to be.
And even though my sister was with me, I missed my mommy so badly, I did
nothing but cry. When they couldn't take another minute of my sobbing, they
shipped me off to Dad's older brother—my sister to another location—where
I'd stay till they got sick of me too. My only memory of that time is having badly burnt hands, after slipping into a tub, as scalding hot water screamed from
the faucet. Water that gave me blisters so bad, I couldn't close my fingers for a
week. And it was there I said over and over again, "But I'm just a little girl."

And right then
you stop talking
stop remembering
when the anxiety of what comes next
gets too big.

Tied to all this is the course I'm taking, with a practicum at a Northampton
pre-school for three- and four-year-olds. I go once a week and as I watch them
chase each other around the playground, my hands get clammy. I get agitat-
ed and have to turn away. Each time I have to observe them, I sleep fitfully
the night before. I don't start making the connection until I speak about my
daughter to my therapist. I hated that age range the most with her, and cringed

at the thought of playing with her back then.

Drinking more than usual at that precious time of her life.

I also notice that the only articles I read in the newspaper anymore are the ones about child molestation and pedophilia. I've given it little thought until right now. The link in these observations is too obvious to ignore.

Driving home from your therapy session
you blurt out something
that nearly veers you off the road.
"Mommy, I need you, he's hurting me"
skids sideways through your lips
you have no control over what you say
it's both terrifying and liberating
all at the same time.

At my next appointment, I share this with my therapist. She looks compassionately at me from her rocking chair. Her brow furrows a bit and that upside down smile she gets when she's feeling bad for me appears. She asks me what I think this all means.

I tell her it happened during that last placement of mine. This deed that's too foggy to nail down. I'd been sent to stay with my sister, at a friend of my parents, where they lived during the war. The only memory I have is being touched in a way I sense was wrong. Its icky-ness oozes from memories too far away to grasp. The perpetrator of this deed is muddled in my whimpering mind.

I'm not sure what to do with this new information, this mass of slime that's been laid in my lap. But I know when I get home, I'll need to lock my bedroom door. With my precious daughter in the house, the steam this disturbing information begins to produce will need to be contained.

It's no wonder the recent love-making with your husband went so badly
that you drank so much through all those other nights of sex
this stuff's been wheedling its way to the surface
ready to break out of its shell
and knock the shit out of anyone
who lays their dirty little hands

on this precious body of yours
and that's when you start to think
you never want to have sex
ever again.

chapter twenty

Desperate Love

I found a one-bedroom apartment in center city, a block and a half from the Schuylkill, on Walnut between 22nd and 23rd. It was a promising third floor walkup that needed work and I was able to get the rent reduced in exchange for doing some painting and resurfacing floors. A short walk to work, it was also close to the old bars I used to frequent.

My parents had recently sold our childhood home, the house where I had my first drink, to relocate themselves to the Jersey Shore, a place my mom had always wanted to live. They were getting rid of things I could use, so I persuaded my youngest brother to help me move the stuff into my place. He said I could pay him in beer, this brother of mine who used to brew his own. This same brother, who partied through much of his life, would take three years of Big House incarceration to finally get him sober.

At least for a while.

I settled into my new digs, spending nights getting used to sleeping alone with no one else around, by numbing myself with frequent trips to a nearby saloon and package store. I also invited Merry, Terry, and Jeanette for dinner. I bought ample bottles of wine to assuage the loss I still felt over their upcoming departure. Why was I so jealous? We weren't a couple, though our label of two-peas-in-a-pod may have had some leading to believe we were. For years, I had pooh-poohed Jeanette's jealousy of Merry and me, her feelings of rejection and being left out was an incredible annoyance. My level of empathy and compassion back then was basically nil. That night, she would take a picture of Merry, Terry, and me, sitting gleefully in my bathtub, after many glasses of wine, all smiles and giggles, like nothing was wrong.

As it turned out

things would only get worse.

To keep up my rent, and lessen the grief of losing Merry and Terry, I picked up catering gigs nearly every weekend, spending more time with, Ron, a commingling the job easily afforded. I'll never forget the night we were out, after an evening of serving the rich and famous, a night we ran into his boyfriend, both of us sure we were at a place we'd never be seen, as we drank more to suppress any guilt that might interfere with the fun we were having. Before the summer was over, I'd get pregnant by this man who swung both ways, this man that I adored and knew I would never have a life with. But as I was unknowingly pregnant with this mostly gay man's child, I would attend a family gathering that would change my life forever.

Merry and I drove our blue VW, which was parked on the street behind the Walnut Street commune where Merry still lived, to East Hampton, New York for a weekend in late July. Aunt Minnie and Uncle Frank were having a reunion, where the family would drive great distances to catch up and drink. These events were always a mixture of laughter and grief. Though I'd had many lovers since my first night with Lenny, more than I'd ever like to claim, seeing him at these gatherings always rekindled that flame, a candle I'd hold for him through a good portion of my life. He'd hastily gotten married two years before, to a woman he'd met on a trip to Europe, to a woman he'd split up with just two years later.

But it was Ed's friend, Rickey, I hooked up with, whom we'd visited years before at his Syracuse apartment, and had since gotten married to another woman named Carol. He recently realized he'd made a mistake and was separated from his wife. We flirted all night and most of the next day, with my cousin joining in on our flirtatious dance. By the second night, he and I'd snuck off to a cot on the porch, when everyone else was tucked in, and spent our first night together, with love-making so intense, even the masses of liquor and pot we'd consumed could not squash the passion.

We fell asleep as one

and in the morning

when I woke up

he was gone.

I questioned others of his whereabouts and discovered he'd snuck off to the beach with my cousin. I wouldn't find out until our ride back to Philly that she'd also hooked up with the same man I'd slept with the night before, on this beach escapade, where a secluded dune was found. The passive-aggression that erupts from too much drinking, often passes on anger that one refuses to deal with directly. And it felt like Merry was passing hers on to me. I had done the same with my sister much of my life, passing it off as humor, but always with an acerbic bite that delivered a punch.

It wasn't long after this trip that I found out I was pregnant. Missing a few periods waved a red flag. I confirmed it by one of those drug store kits, and of course, peed all over my hand, who doesn't, and then had a doctor corroborate the worst, realizing the impregnator could only be my friend, Ron. I knew for sure I could never be a single mom back then, as I was still finding my way through the muck of my meandering life. So I scheduled an appointment with Planned Parenthood to terminate the pregnancy, a decision I had little qualms about making. My drinking was a way of combating the angst and guilt this procedure produced. Ron came with me, propping me up when I seemed ready to fall, and got me through the day, ending with a couple bottles of wine to erase what we'd just done.

A couple weeks later, I got a call from Rickey, saying he couldn't stop think-ing about me, apologizing profusely for going to the beach without me, which I'd made a big thing of that same day. I didn't mention that I knew about his rendezvous with Merry. I wasn't drunk enough for that kind of confrontation, and made plans with him to visit me in Philly for a weekend.

He arrived three weeks later, after talking on the phone almost nightly in the interim, reveling in the similarities of our pasts. His dad had also been hos-pitalized with tuberculosis like my mom, one of the many things that connect-ed us. When I met him at 30th Street station, he came up the escalator, a bou-quet of flowers in his hand, and a duo of tiny Band-Aids on both his cheeks, covering up eruptions that marred his ruddy face. This adolescent-type of vulnerability swept me off my feet, and I became captivated by this man who seemed enchanted with me. My desperation for this kind of connection was a force blinding me to the truth. He was still a married man, who had sex with my cousin the same weekend he had sex with me, a reality I successfully pushed to the back of my mind, soaking up his attention like an old sponge that had withered on the counter too long.

I made him a gourmet dinner of sautéed soft shell crabs and asparagus braised with garlic and white wine, finishing it all with a rich chocolate mousse and a generous dollop of freshly whipped cream for dessert. After a couple of before-dinner gin and tonics, we quickly polished off the first bottle of chardonnay, and then opened a second. We gave little thought to the amount we drank, as we dined on the horizontal roof outside my kitchen window, gazing up at the stars, falling in love with each sip we took.

This was the night I revealed a secret of mine, after much discussion of our parents' failed marriages and their drunken brawls.

I told him, "I think I might be an alcoholic."

He all but laughed at me, covering my hand with his, and telling me with all the self-assurance that I lacked, "I know what alcoholics look like, and you're not one of them."

Looking into his Irish-blue eyes, ready to dive in for a swim, I believed what he said. I was nothing like his drunken mother or father. With that, he pulled out a small wooden box from his shirt pocket, sliding it across the table to my pearly painted fingertips. Inside I found a gold necklace, three strands braided together, perhaps an unspoken apology for his misbehavior with my cousin.

Booze has a way of coloring outside the lines
of making things into something they're not
as my heart bulged inside my chest
stomping out a rhythm I couldn't refuse.

Our weekend consisted of multiple bottles of wine and plenty of sex, of strolls through the city, reveling in each other's company. We compared stories about Ed, the man who introduced us, and all the crazy things he'd done in the years we'd known him. It was a weekend of gazing into each other's eyes, the way new lovers do, burrowing into each other's souls through this optical portal, his far bluer than my own. He was a man who cried through movies, at scenes that also touched something in me, his letting this vulnerable side of himself be seen in my presence enamored me to no end. A man of great sensitivity, he was a teacher who cherished his students, who could make a point I might not agree with, and then easily sway me to his side.

We continued this relationship with nightly calls that lasted for hours. One weekend when he came down, we went to Veteran's Stadium to see the Phillies play the Mets. I'd been a fan since day one, and as usual, they weren't doing well. This night, I was the only Mets fan in a sea of Phillies fanatics. The beer kept coming as the night wore on, and I found myself getting into verbal clashes with people around me, standing with fists drilled into my hips, occasionally raising one into the air to make a point. I sobbed at the end of the game when the Mets lost 2-1.

He'd come down to Philly a few more times, and one night, in an outdoor cafe, over cups of espresso and flaming shots of ouzo, he told me he could see himself spending the rest of his life with me. In the background, *Baker Street* flowed through speakers, a song with a dynamic sax solo at its intro and a chorus that pulled you deeply into its melancholic tale. The lyrics speak of booze, depression, and promiscuous sex that mimicked closely the story of our lives. *"…Well another crazy day, you'll drink the night away, and forget about everything…."* It would become our song, in more ways than one, this song written by a Scotsman who'd one day succumb to the debilitating effects of alcoholism, the irony of it not lost on me now.

I quickly accepted his proposal, as nebulous as it was, and started making plans to relocate to Massachusetts where he lived. *Someone actually wants me for his partner* kept ringing through my head, which caused me to jump in headfirst, without even giving the water a sideways glance.

We made plans for me to move in with him in early November, and just three weeks before I'd make one of the biggest changes of my life, my Aunt Lu suffered another cerebral hemorrhage. This time, a fatal one. My cousin, Jeanette, found her collapsed in their Palmyra home, lying motionless at the foot of her bed. I'd lost contact with my aunt after my uncle died. I pulled away from someone I cared deeply about, as her excessive drinking in the last two years was too hard for me to bear. Her organs were donated at her request, and her cremation was the first I'd ever attend. I remember little of the service we had, with liquor flowing like a rampaging stream, not wanting to get kicked off the raft I was on, as I floated around in the headiness that only early love produces.

Rickey came down for my birthday, just a couple weeks before the move. We dined at a Moroccan restaurant that I chose, where we ordered Bastilla, a sweet and savory flakey-crusted dish we ate with our fingers. And drank lavish amounts of wine as we huddled together atop brightly colored pillows on the majestically carpeted floor. We went to a Halloween party back at the Walnut Street house where I introduced my new love to all my friends. We were dressed as nothing but our happy selves, a couple of lovers who had sworn themselves to each other, who were moving in together, in a town far away from everyone I knew.

My cousin Jeanette remembered this happiness
following her mother's death
and held it close to her heart
a hand grenade ready to explode.

I said good-bye to Merry, my cousin and best friend, whom I'd lost to a friend who'd treated her better than I had. A woman who built her up rather than tear her down, as I often did, falsely propelling my own confidence as this criticism occurred. It's an all too common relational exchange for people like me, one I wouldn't understand the hurtful dynamic of for a number of years to come.

People who drink as much as I did back then, have a difficult time knowing the harm they cause and learning from their mistakes. Instead of feeling the pain that accompanies misdeeds like that, we drink away the hurt, impairing ourselves the insight that comes from feeling the pain.

The big moving day arrived and we rented a U-Haul trailer that we attached to Rickey's car. Merry decided to let me have our VW Beetle that was registered in my name. But when Rickey and I tried to move it out of its parking spot, where it had sat lonely and immobile for a number of months, it wouldn't budge. So we shrugged our shoulders and left it there. We took off for Massachusetts, snuggling close on the bench seat of his hunter green Mustang, waving good-bye to Philly with a six-pack by our side, and headed north to our new life together.

With another 12 years of drinking
before I finally saw the light.

chapter twenty-one

Reeking of Shame

Now that I've uncovered this unsettling stuff from my past, similar things start popping up in this foggy brain of mine. Which leads to more treks into my faulty childhood, back to some playtime at six or seven, after my mother's hospitalization with TB the second time. Having relapsed six months after my youngest brother's birth, she spends another year away from us, a trauma I act out with friends younger than me. I'm the oldest in the group I play with and doctor is a favorite game of ours, sticking bobby pins into little rear ends, I pretend to take temperatures, with doors always closed for this doctorly deed.

Recalling the day I'm tattled on, my mom only recently home from her hospital stay, I listen from another room as she squawks on the phone. The other mother dumps her disgust into my mother's ear, as her words, "I'll have a talk with her," leak into mine. I hide away in the crawl space, only to be found by my finger-pointing mom, shame spitting from fingertips, like bullets from a gun.

Your eyes glue to the floor
as you share this with your therapist.

Since sexual exploration is the topic dujour, I reveal my first attempt at masterbating when I was eleven or so, ironically using a can of beer I get from the fridge to rub myself with, as my sister sleeps in the bed next to mine. This kind of mortal-sinning follows me through high school, when I discover the vibrating pillow my mother uses for her bad back, resulting in satisfaction that comes much quicker than that can of beer. Even though I'm Catholic, with nuns breathing down our necks from fourth to twelfth grade, I never confess this act of pleasure to a priest, sensing this is something private to keep for myself.

And I have no inclination for it now
as all this stuff from the past surfaces
even with the abundant alone time I possess.

I think I'm getting used to being alone. The chatter in my head is still rampaging, though not as forceful as before. I send away for books that relieve some of my fears. My neighbor also lends me titles that seemed to help her. *CoDependent No More* is one she shares. Leafing through the pages, I see myself glaring out at me. *Are you addicted to your husband?* is the question that keeps visiting my brain. The more I read, the more I'm certain the answer is yes.

I take walks in the cornfield adjacent to our house, trying to clear the head that still battles with itself. The geese gather there in fall and their presence comforts me. When the moon is full, my daughter and Rusty go with me. We cross the street and take the dirt road that snakes through the field. Rusty chases critters scurrying between the rows. This becomes a monthly thing, the three of us together in a glow of light that's somewhere between night and day. I become so enamored by this ritual, I write a story about it.

It's the first manuscript I submit to a publisher.

I inquire at the library, where I take out big stacks of picture books, and ask how I might find out more about writing for children. Mrs. Freebourn, our favorite librarian who brings books to my daughter's school for kids to check out, suggests I try Jane Yolen's monthly group held at the Hatfield Library. She critiques other writers' manuscripts with her keen editor's ear. It's where I meet Linda, Nancy, Tom, and Elaine, who will help change my life. I join their writing group that also meets once a month. I yearn to learn the craft, something that stirs up the same kind of passion I used to have for drinking and finding a mate.

I meet with them for the first time at Elaine's, in the Northampton bookbindery run with her husband, and we sit together in the section where they live. I read one of my stories, too naïve to wait until I've nailed down the form. They're kind with their feedback, but that won't last too long. As I continue to write, the more honest critique I'll need.

I spend weekends without my daughter, hunkering down in the computer lab at the college, punching out stories that keep filling my head. Stories that seem to pry open my heart and even heal it a bit. I have no computer at home, and being here makes me feel closer to my husband and daughter. They're only two miles away, doing things without me, carrying on by themselves.

I don't go to visit them, as things have been dubious since our trial weekend away. I'm not sure how I feel right now. Even though we're living apart, my attachment to him is as strong as ever, a compulsion that strips me of any ability to really break free. I'm trapped inside a closet of my own making, unable to find the light switch, no matter how long I grope around in there.

Nights are a mixed bag when my daughter's with her dad. I often make plans with friends, but sometimes dread coming home. The house is a blaring reminder of the emptiness I feel without her here, still in search of replacements to fill the space that drinking and my husband dwelled in so long.

You begin to worry
if she's becoming
a stand-in for him?

My dog is my constant companion on these endless nights of longing, as picking up the phone to make calls is the hardest thing to do. The weight of that phone is a ton in my hand. A truckload of shame still eats away at me, a shame I'd like to unload at the town dump. Instead, it sticks to me like a fly trap of slime, its funk so odiferous, I'm surprised I don't gag from it all. I keep a copy of *Healing the Shame That Binds You* next to my bed. Its author is also in recovery, and though I've studied the chapters like a final exam looms, the shame continues to clog up my veins.

The shame a can of Drano won't begin to touch
which makes it hard to move forward
the steps you take to conquer it never enough.

Speaking of shame, I get a call from my daughter's second grade teacher, asking if I'd mind coming in to see her at school. She needs to talk to me, but wants to do it in person. I feel like a kid being called to the principal's office. I look at her quizzically as she gathers the strength to say what's on her mind. She tells me that my daughter's doing well this year, but she's concerned about something she heard her say. When one of her classmates did some silly thing she hadn't liked, apparently she said, "I'll kill you if you ever do that again." I gasp inside my head and feel my face heating up.

That dirty old shame starts oozing from your pores
you can taste its putrid smell
as her teacher asks where she might have gotten that from
with no reasonable answer coming into view
and you leave the classroom reeking of it
certain you'll need to take another shower when you get home
this thing called shame has a tendency to follow you around
to get its filthy hands into everything you do.

chapter twenty-two

New Kid on the Block

We cruised over the mountain, taking in the glorious Pioneer Valley that emerged below. The thrill of that vista is still with me today. We moved me into his cozy, two-bedroom home, with a dairy farm as our stone's-throw neighbor, set back from the country highway that rambles through the town. I slept poorly that first night, missing the ever-present hum of the city. The silence of this rural setting roared in my ears.

Sometime during my first week, he took me to a local tavern called the Red Basket, just up the street from where I now lived, the bar where Liz Taylor and Richard Burton filmed the roadhouse scene from *Who's Afraid of Virginia Wolf?* Where George, in a jealous rage, attempted to strangle his wife, Martha, exhibiting the perfect example of art imitating life. This infamous place became one of our many hangouts. He introduced me to the owner's son, a gangling young man whose goofiness was an endearing part of his persona, who played a squeezebox to entertain the clientele who came to drink. Rickey signed up for their softball team, which became part of my new social life for years to come.

I settled into this new home, in a town where I had no friends, with a man I hardly knew at the center of my life. I was too naïve to grasp what I'd gotten myself into. Walking down the street with this man, who would audibly gulp when an attractive woman walked by, was a sign I'd stepped into this relationship far sooner than I should have.

My desperate-alcoholic-self was blind to red flags
no matter how many were raised.

After a month or so, a colleague of Rickey's gasped when she heard I had no car, and instructed him to buy me one lickety-split. We bought another Beetle, this one bright orange, for the girl from that part of Jersey, the place where my parents no longer lived. I soon felt a sense of freedom, after staying cooped up in this cozy house too long. I remember the first time I pulled up to the bank, parking beside a pick-up with a steer standing in its bed, a sight that had me laughing for days, reminding me I had left the city for good. I was a country bumpkin now, who missed the life she left behind.

But I was in love and nothing at all seemed to top that
as the constant drinking helped block the grief I felt much of the time.

My first job was at a bar adjacent to where we lived, next to Pure Foods, the grocery store where we bought our essentials. I bartended there for six months or so, a position that seemed to fit me like tight jeans. But I soon grew weary of the obvious alcoholics, who'd sit for hours whining into their drinks, complaining about their wives and husbands who nagged them too much, something that rang too close to my mother and father's rants about each other.

My next stint was at the St. Regis, a family owned restaurant in Northampton that closed a few years after I arrived. I waited tables, but longed to be back in the kitchen, where all the action was, drawn by the artistry of preparing and presenting meals.

Just down the street from where I worked was a bar called Hugo's, a biker kind of joint where die-hards hung out, with a pool table squatting in the back room that made me feel at home. I fit right into this mangy scene, its patrons always appearing down on their luck, ready to battle the next guy who looked at them with an eyebrow aloft. One night, I nearly got pulled into a brawl over a fierce game of pool, some guy ready to clock me, before my paladin stepped in.

Though we liked the bar scenes, we spent much of our time at home finding out about each other, uncovering our pasts over bottles of wine and beer, comparing dysfunctional stories of our younger lives. He had lived with his dad in his later years, before his alcohol abuse led to his death at age 53. He told me about the empty liquor bottles he found hidden in a closet, tumbling out when he opened the door. And how he finally found the nerve to confront him about his drinking, grabbing him by the collar, throwing him against the wall, shaking his father till he broke down in tears.

An image that gripped me in my dreams.

I missed my friends terribly, and called them often, talking for hours tipsy on wine. When I wasn't seeking relief from long-distance friends, I'd curl up on Rickey's lap like a troubled toddler, getting needs met that were unsatisfied in my younger years, my continuous desire for affection, a bottomless pit.

On weekends when I didn't work, we hopped in the Mustang and took off, scouting around western Mass like two explorers, high on pot and stoked from beer. This fed my adventurous spirit, appeased my migrant soul. With the stereo blasting Earth, Wind and Fire or The Spinners, we'd flit around the hill towns with no destination in mind, in pursuit of quaint drinking holes we could always find.

I remember a night we ended up at a tavern in Otis that had a piano player with a mic. He played show tunes, which was right up my ally, and after a few gin and tonics, I asked if I could sing. I grabbed the mic and belted out songs from *The Sound of Music*, reminding me of my cousin, Merry, whom I deeply missed.

My need for attention was always at the core of such displays
my middle-child-syndrome showed up frequently.

Six or so months after my arrival, I answered an ad for a sous chef's position at Beardsley's. An upscale café restaurant around the corner from where I worked, it was owned by a wealthy young man who bought the place on a whim and snorted his profits up his nose. I'd spend a week at home, rehearsing for my culinary audition, preparing various recipes to try out on the chef. My chicken, sausage, and mushroom dish got me hired and placed in charge of Sunday brunch, making oodles of hollandaise to ladle over poached eggs for this always packed service.

I became friends with Tom Foxx and his wife, Pennie, who worked in the kitchen as a team. Tom was a retired NYC-cop-turned-chef in mid-life and 25 years older than his young bride. His daughter, Elsa, the same age as his wife, worked alongside them. Pennie and I laughed at the same things, and I immediately hit it off with this woman who spoke fluent French, a vibrant, hilarious lady who'd be my first real friend in my New England home.

My second audition was for a theater group called ECTA, a local community troupe that performed in the next town over, the small city where Rickey's wife still lived. I'll never forget the day we drove to her house knowing full well she wasn't there, a house they'd rented before splitting up, to rustle-up an old brass bed, one that was foolishly painted over. We put it in our guest room, so visitors who came to stay had a decent place to sleep. We rationalized the deed, as it was just sitting on the porch, wasting away, needing to be used.

I shrugged my shoulders, an accomplice to the act.

The daily intake of alcohol allowed me to do such things, for as soon as any feelings of guilt or shame arose, a drink (or four) pushed the angst into some hidden psychic closet, securing the lock, where it wouldn't be seen or heard from, ever again. Of course, that's what we serious drinkers tell ourselves. Those repressed feelings usually turn up in something else we do.

I auditioned with ECTA for the musical *South Pacific*. They were looking for their Nellie Forbush, a character I'd always wanted to play, a singing role made for Mary Martin's range, and certainly not mine. An artistic and talented couple named John and Atea Ring were running the auditions, and wound up casting me in the part. Atea, a woman who became both a sister and a mother to me, gave voice lessons and took me on as a student, teaching me how to master this challenging role. We performed at the Williston-Northampton School Theater, a place where their children were schooled, a far cry from the Catholic education both Rickey and I received.

I pulled off the part, singing and rehearsing nightly with Rickey standing in for Emile de Becque, in a production where I washed my hair each night on stage for its 12-performance run. And when singing "I'm in Love with a Wonderful Guy," it came with an open heart for the guy I lived with, finding it difficult to kiss my leading man, as I waited to drink until after the curtain had closed.

Our first year together was a mix of honeymooning and grief, both of us grieving losses of lives we left behind, mine far away, his close at hand. Only months before we were reunited at my aunt's July reunion, he had left his wife, a second separation in their short marriage. The first time, he walked out the door with no explanation at all, leaving her stunned and confused, too young and deeply wounded by his own childhood to know how to proceed with any dignity or respect.

He often slept late, paralyzed by depression, rising only when he had to get up, his classes at the college calling him to duty, shaking him out of his confusion and funk. At night we drank, when depression seemed to dissolve, the fermented sugars of our concoctions a momentary lift. Then waking the next day with the same depression he failed to kick, descending once again, as the cycle of unresolved issues rewound themselves for their next turn at bat.

That first year he bought me a vacuum and a sewing machine, practical gifts I accepted with a smile, clearly defining my role in our household. I was too unaware and in love to even consider the notion. I quickly found out that our house could be vacuumed without ever unplugging that dirt-sucking appliance.

It was also a year of single red roses bought on whims: there was always one in the house. It was a year of tasting wines, recording the ones we tried, setting us apart from other drinkers, a superior status we would always try to seek. On my first birthday with him, he cooked a scrumptious dinner served with a pricey bottle of Dom Perignon, and a cake fashioned from six cannoli, accompanied by a '67 Château d'Yquem, which I puked up before night's end.

It was also another year of getting pregnant, and in a haze of confusion and grief, I decided again not to have the baby. A decision assuaged by the soothing comfort of alcohol.

Copious amounts of it.

As time ticked on, I pushed him to get a divorce, causing friction that hadn't been there, applying pressure that wasn't well received. We fought like our parents, fueling our arguments with more and more booze. Gin and tonics, margaritas, martinis, and the ever-present beer stoked the furnace of fights, resolving nothing, as we walked away, licking our wounds. I longed to be a Sadie, as Barbra Streisand sang its praises in *Funny Girl*, but that would never happen as long as he was still legally attached to someone else.

One night, we got into such a fierce argument, his hands were suddenly wrapped around my neck. He had a crazed look in his eyes, similar to the look of Montauk Roger, squeezing the anger through his fingers, until realizing the extent of his rage. It scared us both. I told him if he ever laid a hand on me again, I was out of there. He never did.

With the subject of marriage looming large in my head, I found out through the family grapevine that my cousin, Jeanette, was getting married to a sweet guy she started dating while I still lived in Philly. Rumor had it she was not inviting me to the wedding, still mad at me for displaying such first-love-euphoria so soon after her mother's death.

To soften the blow of this baffling exclusion, my sister invited us to Panama, to come anytime we wanted, come soon she always said, her homesickness assuaged by family visits. We decided to go for Christmas, the time of year I missed them most. We stayed for 10 days, flitting from party to party, as their life in the Canal Zone consisted of entertaining and comforting each other with lavish dinner parties, unlike ones we'd ever see back home.

The food was always exquisite, the booze flowed non-stop.

Being with them was just the salve I needed. They rented a cottage overlooking the ocean, where peacocks roamed around like squirrels do here. Our days were spent playing in the ocean or touring the countryside, our nights eating out in an open thatched-roof hut, overlooking the sea.

I cried when I left them

saying good-bye is always difficult for me

ordering multiple drinks on the plane home helped allay the grief.

The following year, my cousin Jeanette, who had excluded me from her wedding and was also a middle child like myself, contracted Ewing Sarcoma. A usually fatal bone cancer, it's notably diagnosed in children far younger than my 28-year-old cousin. It would send a lightening bolt of grief through our family once again. And it was around this time that Rickey and I were making plans to travel, Paris at the heart of our fantasy, wanting to see more of the world before we actually settled down. We longed to go to Ireland to search out family, to visit our roots, to feed my need for adventure, which filled me with more confusion and grief.

I wrote Jeanette numerous letters, attempting to help heal the bitterness she carried in her heart towards me, giving her as much compassion as I could muster, considering the resentment she had for me back then. Years ago, I had taken her sister from her, the one she relied on for advice and strength, this younger cousin who used food to comfort herself, fighting with it for years. This same cousin, who, at one time in our lives, even idolized me. The treatments she now received were making her sicker, eating her up like some parasite lurking inside. Anytime I called, she'd bark at whatever I said, angry at the world for what she had to endure, making it difficult to call again. Rickey and I continued making plans, and booked our flight to Ireland through my cousin's deteriorating health, too far away from her to really make a difference was always my rationale.

I had also recently switched jobs, following Tom and Pennie to a new restaurant in Springfield called Lincoln Hall, bought and renovated by an auto-body guy named Carl, a compactly built Lebanese man with close ties to the local mafia. It was there a young blonde sous chef of Tom's, wooed his wife away from him, splitting their marriage in two and tearing at our hearts.

The months before leaving on our trip, I took French lessons from Pennie, in exchange for the bottles of wine I brought along to our sessions. She had moved to an apartment in the town where Rickey's wife still lived. We drank the wine, as she tried to instill the basics of conversational French into my somewhat tipsy head.

Alcohol has a way of doing that
fogging up a brain, eradicating its cells
an eradication that wouldn't cease
until I made the decision to stop.

chapter twenty-three

Glued Back Together

Though I still go to 12 Step meetings, I've stopped going every day. I bring my shame to the ones I attend. The best way of ridding myself of this ucky stuff is talking about it, where heads nod in unison, bearing witness to my soul and my shit. I listen to others, with the same sort of gunk on their tongues, as they take turns unloading theirs. We give each other undivided attention, something none of us got as children. The same attention I get from the therapist I see. I feel cleansed and validated when I leave the rooms.

Ready to plod through another day without a drink.

In an effort to prop myself up, I hang slogan's and affirmations around my house. They go in places that are visible, on mirrors and cabinets, and hang on closet doors.

Life supports me.

I am in the process of positive change.

I trust my inner wisdom.

My future is glorious.

I love and approve of myself.

And my favorite, sitting on my nightstand, one I read before I go to sleep:

I trust the process of life

Everything I need is always provided

I am safe

The universe takes care of me.

I also screw up the courage to apply to substitute teach. Working at my daughter's school will provide me additional time with her. I get called the next week. As a lump rises in my throat, I try to trust the process of life and say yes to the request. I'm assigned to the other second grade at her school. I can't stop thinking about that class of eighth graders, who gobbled me up and spit me out years ago. The amount of wine I drank at the end of that day is no longer available for me to unwind.

Could second graders possibly be as bad as those pubescent kids were?

I nervously check out the lesson plans. They make little sense to me as they shake wildly in my hands. I soon realize I have no idea how to control a group of 23 seven-year-olds. What have I gotten myself into quickly crosses my mind. I seem to wind them up more than calm them down. A teacher or two poke their heads in the door to make sure everything's okay. I'm exhausted at the end of the day, but feel accomplished for putting myself out there again.

I know I can't rely on my husband anymore. He seems to be pulling himself further and further away from me and my new way of life. Though we still see each other once a week, our dates aren't going well. The chasm between us grows wider each time we're together. We try being friends, but the lack of sex thing has become onerous, like some gnarly beast sitting between us in the car.

You need way more time to heal that part of you
a parcel of time he has little or no patience for
holding hands is the best that you can do
something he's not really into anymore.

I discover another family reunion is being held that summer. This one in New Jersey, at my cousin Liz's house. Though a part of me longs to see every-one, the thought of exposing my still-developing and wobbly recovering self to their judgments and criticisms, feels unsafe and out of the question. When I turn down the invitation, I know there'll be grumbling about me in the family wings.

Not long after this, Lenny calls to ask if he can visit with his lovely young wife. My new self, who considers things before committing to an answer, tells him I need to check my schedule, can he call me back. When he does, I turn him down.

"It just isn't a good time for me, Len."

"What do you mean it isn't a good time, we just want to visit?" The backlash I get brings up a torrent of guilt, but it doesn't make me change my mind.

You've learned feeling guilty is a sign of good self-care.
You know you'll be the talk of the family for years to come.
You're growing used to this new status.
You may even grow to like it someday.

My sister also wants to visit. She calls and leaves a message, something about going to New Jersey to see our mom, and wants to stop by on her way back home. I haven't seen or talked with her in ages. This message stirs up feelings I pushed down for years. But now that I'm not drinking, I'm being forced to deal with them. I've worked on some of this with my therapist, hashing out bits of anger in her office, but I'm not sure I'm ready to be with my sister. I don't know how to be anything but my passive-aggressive self with her. My anger comes out sideways, in the form of sarcastic put-downs disguised as jokes, ones she's always laughed at, and the way we've dealt with my envy and jealousy of her for years.

But she's sober now
and you wonder if
she'll still think you're funny
because you have a strong sense
you're not.

I wait a few days before calling her back. She's so happy to hear my voice, it scares me. Those feelings I spent years drinking away, wiggle to the surface again. And before I know what I'm doing, I agree to a visit.

This means I'll have to clean my house. I haven't changed so much as to let that compulsion go. I still need my home to be tidy before anyone steps inside. Especially my sister, who, when we were teens, came into my third-floor bedroom once a week to straighten things up and sniff the pits of my uniform blouses to make sure they smelled okay.

When she arrives, I feel myself clam up. I'm not sure how to act with her now, as my anger bubbles to the surface. I push it down with chocolate, a tasty but poor substitute for the booze that always worked so well. My daughter is a good distraction, but when she goes to bed, it's just the two of us, awkward and tense, and I can't push the feelings down any more. We're out on the porch, candles lit, sipping glasses of club soda spiked with cranberry juice—a paltry replacement for the wine we once loved to drink—when I begin to spew my stuff.

"You were always Mommy's favorite, always working your ass off to maintain that status. And you always did so well in school…do you have any idea how hard that was to follow? And of course, now you're married to a guy who makes more freaking money than the president." I go on and on, you-ing her to death, my voice getting louder with each resentment I spill.

My sister just sits there
doesn't say a word
taking in all the junk I'm spewing.
Until she looks me squarely in the eyes and says this
"I'm sorry for ever being born."
Spoken with a depth of sincerity that splits open my resentful heart.

We both stay silent, as a light June breeze whispers through the screens. And then the crying and hugging begins. My sister, who's been a second mother to me, has uttered seven inconceivable words.

Words that even in my deepest hours of resentment
I could never imagine thinking.
Words that say she finally understands.
Words that begin to heal that decades-old wound
Like a small wave rippling through my heart.

chapter twenty-four

Dingle, Paris, and the Drive From Hell and Back

W e left for Europe in early June. Arriving in London, we traversed by train through Wales and on to Dublin, where we rented a car. While traveling this verdant country, I thought of my cousin, who was close to dying back home. I buried my guilt in pints of Guinness, downing the dark lager with far too much vigor. One night I got so drunk, a bad case of hiccups ensued. Everything I tried to rid myself of this inebriated upshot failed. Until someone suggested a knife in a glass of water, its handle resting on my temple, as I sipped the clear drink.

Never seeing the irony of a knife to the temple to relieve my pain.

Rickey fit into Ireland like spring lamb in stew, and was often taken for a native son. After crossing the country from Dublin to Galway, we arrived in Dingle, a quant little town with 56 pubs to its name. We felt we were home. My guilt about Jeanette traveled beside me while I tried my best to enjoy our stay. This was a new thing for us, being with each other 24/7, both of us possessing distinctly different viewpoints about the money we'd budgeted for the trip. I wanted to preserve our funds so we could extend our stay, while Rickey cashed traveler's checks like they were winning lottery tickets.

We found a bed and breakfast run by a kindly Mrs. O'Connell overlooking the magnificent Slea Head cliffs, the place I'd skinny-dip in a chilly 50 degree sea, on the beach where *Ryan's Daughter* was filmed. Our nights were spent in pubs, throwing back pints with Irish farmers, who cultivated potatoes on this part of the peninsula and conversed in Gaelic that was unintelligible to us. We spent our last night at the westernmost pub in Europe, with a red-faced farmer playing Irish tunes on his squeezebox, while high-spirited students jigged around us. After a few pints of stout, I joined right in. The next day, we raced across the southern coast to sunny Rosslare, to catch our overnight ferry to Le Havre, which only ran once a week. With us was an American, who we picked up hitch-hiking and who drove our rental back to Dublin Airport, where she herself was headed.

The voyage across a choppy Irish Sea on board the *St. Patrick*, our hotel for this night, was 20 hours long. After digging into some yummy Irish stew, a meal we never finished, we were confined to our cabin for the remainder of the trip. This Vietnam vet, who sailed nine terrifying months in Southeast Asian seas aboard an ammunition ship in the midst of that disreputable war, was glued to his bed with a bad case of seasickness. A condition I'd rib him about for years to come.

A train from Le Havre whisked us to Paris, the city of our dreams. We stayed in a quiet pension called Hotel Plaisant in the heart of the 5th Arrondissement, with bidets in all the toilettes, and flower boxes attached to every balcony overlooking tiny rues. The fragrance of fresh-baked baguettes and rich roasted coffee roused us each morning. At night we dined in cozy bistros, with tumblers of Lillet Blanc before dinner and bottles of the finest French wines with our meals. I was ensconced in epicurean heaven, my romance with great food and wine in sync with my soul, ready to move here at the slightest suggestion.

We continued our fighting, finding ourselves nit-picking about little things now. My insecure self erupted at too many photos he'd taken of chic French women. A photoshoot of young models posing at the Tuileries fountain was the source of one of my irrational tirades. Our disputes over money reached a crescendo at an outdoor café beneath the Arc de Triomphe, when after a lunchtime bottle of wine, I pushed back my chair, yelling things I can't recall, and stomped away, ready to throw in the towel and go home.

It was the turning point in our trip.

Ten non-stop days together was a bit much for both of us.

We needed a good fight to release some claustrophobic steam.

We left Paris shortly after, in the pale green Citroën 2cv we reserved from home. It was a quirky little car with a sunroof that rolled back like a sardine can and a gearshift extending from the dashboard. It was a car neither of us knew how to drive, a car that would eventually escort us into the Alps, on a terrifying venture we had no idea was coming, as we pulled out of the rental garage with a near-empty tank of gas, fretting over each new turn we made. Finally finding a gas station, Rickey fumbled through our francs and ended up paying too much. We were grateful for the attendant's honesty, who returned the overpayment and sent us on our journey.

We found our way out of Paris and headed straight to Épernay, where grapes for champagne are grown, stopping for bottles of vin ordinaire along the way. We eventually settled into the Hotel de La Cloche, after an extravagant dinner that featured a couple bottles of that local sparking wine. It was at this quirky hotel I had a spiritual experience I'll never forget.

We'd come back from a day of exploring the region, driving through vineyards dripping with grapes, passing bottles of wine back and forth as we wove through this wealth of scenery. Relaxing in our room, snacking on crusty bread, saucisson, and the chevre we'd picked up, a feeling came over me, like something had whispered its way through the room. The sheer curtains on the windows that framed a close view of the Église Notre-Dame cathedral, fluttered on this still and breezeless day. I felt my cousin's presence, as a shiver drifted down my spine, and I knew in that instant she had died, breaking down into sobs, certain her spirit had come to say good-bye.

I found out upon returning home
she had passed away
two days before this happened.

We moved on to Beaune, five hours of country driving with our top rolled back, as fields of mustard, lavender, and poppies painted the landscape, made even more vibrant by the vin ordinaire we eagerly drank. We picnicked while motoring through towns and fields that dotted this lush country, a ritual we coined "car-nics" just for this trip, our love of crusty bread, chunks of gooey cheeses and firm sausages, washed down with wine, always with wine.

We checked into a little hotel in this old French city just south of Dijon, in an ancient stucco building I grew to love, with all the same grandmotherly furnishings that were here when the owner's wife was born, who kept parrots that squawked night and day. The innkeeper and owner, Monsieur Rousseau, claimed quite loudly in no uncertain terms after we asked for a room with an adjoining bathroom, *"Ne bain, ni douche!"* This was a phrase I was familiar with, which he repeated numerous times, as if these weary travelers he stood before were hard of hearing.

Which meant, we'd have to go down the hall to wash and pee.

Before we left on our trip, Tom and Pennie Foxx, who'd lived in France a year and a half before they were married, insisted we dine at Alain Chapel's. He was an early innovator of nouvelle cuisine, and owner of a three-starred Michelin restaurant bearing his name in the small village of Mionnay, one that Tom and Pennie had dined at numerous times. I was nervous about this excursion, as I'd never been to a restaurant of this status, unsure of how to act, let alone how to eat. The fact that our French was so limited multiplied my nerves, though Rickey had done much of the speaking for us. My two years of high school French, plus Pennie's wine-filled lessons, did little to assuage my complete lack of confidence.

When we walked into the restaurant spruced to the max, flowers bedecked every nook of its tasteful decor, while a team of waist-coated servers stood like guards at various stations. I was sure they were eyeing each misstep we were about to take. Sweat seeped from my pits, as water was served from highly polished pitchers into majestic goblets that sat beside our place settings. The tables were set so perfectly, with more utensils than we'd ever use, I was afraid to touch anything. Which is exactly what Rickey did, when he pawed some antique crockery sitting atop the mantle, just within reach. Wanting to slap him on the wrist for making this atypical gesture, a stern-looking server came over and chastised him for his behavior. Our bar tab nearly equaled our food bill. A bottle of Puligny Montrachet and two Poire Williams was all we could afford.

Though we immensely enjoyed our food and drink, the dining experience was a tad too formal for our liking, and we were glad to bid this nerve-wracking experience adieu. After taking a morning run together, something we did regularly to stave off lurking demons, desperately trying to prove to ourselves we were not becoming our parents, we checked out of our hotel, packed up our Citroën with its top rolled back and car-nic in place, and headed toward the Alps.

We landed in the foothills, in the commune of Séez, a French town surrounded by snow-capped mountains not far from the Swiss border, and checked into the Hotel Malgovert. It was a charming rustic-looking inn that walked straight from the pages of Johanna Spyri's *Heidi*. The proprietress immediately told us of her vacation in the states, in Nyack, New York, the village where I was born, an unexpected coincidence we drank to that night.

The next day we stocked up on food and wine and headed into the mountains. Checking out of the hotel with no destination in mind, planning to land where our car would take us, we switched back and forth, getting dizzy as we climbed. Looking at the map, we decided to shoot for Italy, following D902 over the Alps, the quickest way from here to there.

Or so we thought.

It was June, the season of avalanches, and as we chugged higher, we found the road narrowing, littered with boulders and shale. There was no guardrail to protect us from a slide over the steep precipice, a deadly drop to the valley below. And worst of all, we were without a sufficient supply of vin ordinaire to see us through this impulsive decision we made. Both of us were so scared, even the steering wheel began to sweat.

At one point, we approached a mound of boulders so large and rocks so deep, to wend our way around them meant the right hand tires, on my side of the car, were centimeters from the edge. Our stomachs lurched as we inched our way around, both of us praying we'd live to see another day. Sweat trickled down the sides of our faces as we continued our climb. These two madcap adventurers were too foolhardy to even think about waving a white flag in retreat.

Besides it was too late to go back

as there was nowhere to turn our Citroën around.

It took us two hours to go two switch-backing miles. When we finally reached the summit of Col de I'Iseran, the highest paved pass in the Alps, at an elevation of 9,088 feet, the snow on its crest was as high as a two story house, where a team of alpine plows were working diligently to clear the road ahead.

An impassable mountain road we'd not be traveling down anytime soon.

After a half-hour of catching our breath, wolfing down chevre on chunks of crusty bread, taking off the edge with swigs from our last bottle of vin ordinaire, we took pictures of the massive snow, amazed by its 20 foot depth as summer officially neared. We switched places, with me in the driver's seat, as Rickey's nerves were frayed to pieces, his stomach in knots and sorely needing to settle down. I drove us back down the mountain from whence we came, my hands gripping the wheel so tight my knuckles turned white, creeping like snails in a race, another two-hour drive that only a few bottles of wine could erase at trip's end.

We found a quant mountain pension to recover in, where roosters crowed at the hint of dawn, and a young boy, his grandfather, and their trusty sheep dog herded cows down alpine lanes, the bells around their necks a symphony to our ears. We stayed for two nights in this quiet setting, soothing our jangled nerves, extensively tattered from our misguided tour.

We were still hell bent on getting to Italy, if only for a quick stay in the town of Turin, which awaited near the end of the snow-covered mountain pass we couldn't take. We arrived late at night and checked into a hotel where a group of young people were watching James Cagney on TV, speaking his lines in Italian, a sight and sound to behold. We only stayed the night and left in the morning for the Med.

We discovered an idyllic hotel on the Côte d'Azur called the Corniche d'Or, with a room gazing out at the Mediterranean Sea. A bottle of champagne was the only thing that would do, as we popped the cork, drinking in the sea, before having dinner in a restaurant where bouillabaisse was served, a meal truly authentic in this part of the world. After two glorious days of runs along the coast and bottles of wine from local grapes, we drove west towards Aix, where we came upon a roller coaster in the middle of the woods in the south of France. We stopped at the OK Corral and rode the Wild Mouse, a roller coaster bursting with memories of my childhood summers at the Seaside Heights boardwalk on the Jersey Shore.

Before leaving on our trip, Rickey's face had broken out again, and one of our friends had given him a topical cream she thought might help. He'd been dabbing it on each day, sometimes more than once, but instead of healing, it seemed to be getting worse. After our trip through the Alps, with the numerous applications in hopes of a cure, blisters were popping out all over his face, a modified version of smallpox that was difficult to take in. He had a hard time meeting the eyes of whoever we met, his shame a knife twisting deep in my heart. Similar to the shame I lugged around for years, though I didn't know it then, shame that only copious amounts of booze (and drugs) could squelch.

We worked our way south and discovered a town northwest of Aix called Saint-Rémy-de-Provence, the town where Nostradomus was born, and where Van Gogh spent his most prolific years, living in the Saint-Paul-de-Mausole Asylum, where he committed himself after cutting off his ear. He created 143 oil paintings while he was there, *Starry Night* being one of his acclaimed asylum works.

We stayed, of course, at the Hotel Van Gogh, a charming inn with reproductions of his paintings scattered about, a still life of sunflowers on the wall in our room. We sat in our small and fairly priced chamber one rainy Sunday afternoon, buzzed from vin ordinaire, gazing out the window trying to see the world as Vincent saw it, sketching the junipers that stood guard along the side of the stone building. We toured the town, with its fountains gurgling, as cars and mopeds buzzed around. I bought a peasant skirt in one of the small shops, with yards of printed cotton and tiny bells jingling on its roped belt.

Fit for the gypsy in me.

We were short of time; our flight back home was in a few days. I'll never forget the small pension we found on our way back to Paris. La Chaumière was nestled along the L'Allier River, where we dined on fresh trout, caught that day from the stream we could see from our room. Served to us by a waitress who gazed on Rickey's blistered face with compassionate eyes, a kindness he'd always be grateful for. Our breakfast of coffee in a bowl, with baguettes on the side, was something we chuckled about the rest of the day.

We stayed two more days in Paris, in our cozy hotel, drinking more of the outstanding wines we could never get back home, leaving this city of lights with great memories to carry with us. I flew home on a high, only to return to the news of my cousin's death. Taken from us at such a young age, it was a grief I continued to contain, pushing it down like all the other feelings that liquor smothers.

My ever-increasing need for alcohol marched on
that intoxicating substance I persistently required
for a number of years to come.

chapter twenty-five

Help to Heal

As things get better between my sister and me, things get worse with my husband. He's starting to bluster about the money he gives me, angry about the bills he continues to pay. An agreement he made at a therapy session, after his staggering announcement he was moving out on Mother's Day.

His resentment is a clue he's turned another corner
a sign that he's heading a different way.

He sends me a letter about my car insurance that's still on his policy, a premium he plans to deduct from my support check, his rage singeing the paper it's written on. I now have to remind him to write the check for me, the funds that support the beautiful child I know he loves.

His passive-aggressive ways force me to feel his fury.

He has stopped seeing our therapist, who we've been meeting with separately to resolve our individual issues, before working on our marriage any further. He's started to see another therapist I know nothing about, working on an issue I'm still in the dark over. Something I'll find out about soon enough.

Something, of course, that will rip you to pieces.

I continue my course load in grad school, working on projects that power my brain. I'm wrestling with three more practicums. One is an early intervention course, where I observe and trail a four-year-old with cerebral palsy, who I work with once a week. Along with two other field experiences in a Holyoke kindergarten and second grade. I work diligently on lesson plans, picking frogs as my theme, attempting to make up for that dismal undergraduate student-teaching semester that issued me a pitiful C. I bend over backwards with activities and materials I hope these kinder kids will like. I even bake a frog-shaped cake, displaying my skill as a baker, the business I manage with school and recovery.

I start writing letters to my inner child, something I learn at a meeting I attend. Working with these young kids, many from dysfunctional backgrounds similar to mine, reminds me of the injured child that still resides in me, who continues to bleed from the inside out. I write her letters in my journal, little love notes from the aspiring-to-be-an-adult version of myself.

I meet a guy at my Sunday meeting, who calls his inner child sweetheart, an inspiration for this letter writing I've begun. He leaves messages for his kidself on his home phone. He calls from work, asking how his day went and says, "I love you" to himself, an act of loving kindness his father never performed. He reminds me of my first lover, Lenny, sometimes a little too much. I connect with him on many levels and grow closer to him each time I'm in his company. I flirt with him more than I should and send out the wrong kind of message from my asexual self. Listening to my body is a new thing for me. Sex when drinking was a misguided illusion of love, an opaque window that frequently slammed in my face.

There's hundreds of losses that need time to heal.

So I respectfully, but directly nudge him away.

Painful to do without the aid of a drink.

I spend more time on my writing and join an organization called SCBW(I) that supports children's book writers still learning the craft. And people like Jane Yolen, who long ago mastered the art of writing for kids. I muster the nerve to send out my first submission, that story I wrote about walking in the moonlight with my daughter and dog. I call it OUR MOON WALKS, a picture book manuscript that's close to my heart.

Other writers tell me I'll need enough rejections to wallpaper my bathroom, before gleaning the acceptance I long to achieve. I hurry the process by sub-mitting to five different publishers. Each day I scurry to my mailbox, certain there'll be good news inside the black metal box that salutes the postman, as he beeps and waves driving by. A month or so later, a flurry of rejections march to my door, all delivering the same woeful news.

Thank you for submitting your work.
We are sorry that it is not right for our list. We
appreciate your letting us consider it, and
we wish you success in placing it elsewhere.

It will take nine more years to get my first children's book accepted, by a New York publisher with a resounding reputation. In the meantime, I contin-ue collecting rejections.

I'm committed to a career for the first time in my life.

I share this news with my husband, who feigns happiness for this new call-ing of mine. His real feelings get revealed in comments like, "You need to get a paying job." His issues around money balloon everyday.

This weighs heavy on you
causing a war to wage inside your head.
At night you toss and turn
sleeping soundly but a dream these days
waking often in the grip of asthma
the uncertainty of your future
a vice around your fragile lungs.

My new friend, Sue, persuades me to see a homeopath, thinking it might help to heal my breathing. I listen to her, as I'm open to alternative ways to repair myself. I start a relationship with a homeopathic doctor, one I'll have for many years.

One who will heal far more than asthma.
One who will help to heal your heart.

chapter twenty-six

Wedding Day Blues

Life back in the states seemed anticlimactic after our trip to Europe. The transition to ordinary life felt tedious to me. I'd hunt for wines we tasted on our adventure, searching for liquor marts selling hard-to-find labels, embracing the wine connoisseurs we'd become. Passing a liquor store without stopping in seemed unimaginable at the time.

I started pushing Rickey harder to get a divorce. With no children or joint property, it seemed like an easy procedure, though you'd hardly know it by the way we consumed.

Our weekends were spent dining out and visiting local taverns. One of those times, we met a lively couple at Packard's, one of our many haunts in Northampton, who enticed us with a gram of coke they happened to have. And without giving it much thought, we invited them back to our home. We partied all night, staying up doing lines of cocaine, with shots of tequila after the buzz wore off. These people we hardly knew wanted to swap partners, inviting us into their world of open relationships, something they were obviously comfortable with and eager for us to try. As high as I was, I declined their invitation, and was miffed Rickey seemed keen to join in the switch. They ended up staying the night, sleeping off the debauch in our guest room, all of us feeling the strained taste of awkwardness, crawling out of bed the next day.

We kept visits with our parents to the required holidays, the mere act of seeing them was always a momentous chore. I grew to hate upstate trips to see his mom, as Rickey spent much of the time there sleeping, the mire of confusion he felt about her deeper than I knew back then. I remembered him mentioning her slipping into bed with him, in her drunken stupors, when he was a boy.

One memorable weekend, my parents came to visit. They were significantly wasted when they arrived and the anger in their eyes was palpable, as the rage they were feeling filled the air. They told the story of their ride to see us, a bottle of vodka on the seat between them, and with tears pooling his aging eyes, my dad related how my mom had hit him with that bottle while speeding down the Mass Pike on their way for the family visit. Though I don't remember the specifics of the fight, as the weekend staggered along, the story kept replaying itself, a broken record that no one would change, until we finally mustered the nerve to ask them to leave. To tolerate another minute of their unhappiness, their mess of a marriage, seemed impossible to bear.

Despite all this, I still wanted to get married. After the divorce was finalized, I pushed for a wedding. And the more I pushed, the more we drank. Even so, we always appeared to be functional, taking runs every day and working at jobs we both loved, making sure our drinking never got in the way of executing our duties as professionals.

I finally told Rickey if he didn't marry me, I would leave. It was a bottom line I wasn't sure I could keep, but I delivered the message with the assurance a few bottles of beer helped me declare, giving him six months to make up his mind. He came through a week before deadline. We'd get married in Cape Hatteras, the place we were going for that year's vacation. It was not the wedding I'd dreamed of having, more like a shotgun event, with me holding the weapon, pointing it at my husband-to-be.

On our way to North Carolina, we stopped at my parents' home in New Jersey. Drinking helps hide the hatchet that needs burying, and the sting of their last visit was safely in the closet with all the other stuff, bulging by now from sheer volume. After trying on a few of my mother's dresses we thought could work for the occasion, I ended up borrowing a two-piece mint-green-polyester-outfit, a pathetic ensemble to wear for the ceremony.

Sadly, that's how desperate I was.

We were staying at a small bungalow owned by a colleague of Rickey's, a cozy house on the water's edge. We got married in Manteo, a town on Roanoke Island not far from the honeymoon cottage, in the city clerk's office inside town hall. Before the ceremony, we drove frantically in search of a florist, as I yearned for a bouquet to alleviate the angst of this slapdash affair. We settled on a corsage, a leftover relic from their high school's grad week, which seemed fine with me, as sadly, I'd never been to prom. We needed a witness, and the only person we could snag was a bashful woman in the Water Works Office, who agreed to stand up for us, staring at the floor the entire time.

A few moments later we were hitched and after shaking hands with the few that were there, we headed straight for a restaurant overlooking the bay, one we'd picked out on our way over, where we ordered two martinis to wash down the day. The sadness we felt was palpable. Sitting in this restaurant, downing our drinks, surrounded by people we didn't know. I had pushed for this, and the only way I could get this recently divorced man to marry me was staring me in the face, as I imagined a large chef's knife stabbing at my heart. After a meal of pity and grief, this newly married couple went back to the cottage and drank two bottles of champagne.

All by themselves.

Sometime that week, we rode our bikes through the pouring rain, pedaling away sadness down Route 12. We crossed over the windswept Bonner Bridge that connects the islands, and headed to the town of Salvo, some 20 miles away. We found a cozy tavern to warm up and dry out. As veterans of the bar scene, it provided the comfort we craved.

Being married meant bigger things awaiting. We both knew we wanted children, and realized we were outgrowing this tiny home of ours, the house you could vacuum without pulling the plug. Though we'd expanded to the basement, where we kept our wood-burning stove, we needed more room and went on the search for a bigger house. We contacted Tim Sullivan, who had brokered the deal on our current home, and who orchestrated a transaction people only dream of making.

We found a house on Russellville Road, a few miles from where we presently lived. An old place built in the early 1800s, it was once owned by Connecticut architect Walter Crabtree, who spent his summers there. Attached to its dark cedar shakes was a plaque saying, Benomi Coleman 1817, the original owner of this historic place. It sat on top of the hill, adjacent to the cornfield that Myke Searle owned, who lived a few houses down from it, and was the perfect setting for starting a new life. With almost seven acres of land, it was on the market for a song.

This now-married couple had found their new home.

The owner was looking to downsize, as the upkeep of this five-bedroom, two-fireplace house was draining his pockets. The work it required was too much for him to do. He took a look at our cozy cape and saw it as the perfect size for him and his three kids, and as we shook our heads at the notion of them squeezing into that wee home of ours, we made the deal. We bought his monstrosity of a house, with all its history and drafty rooms, and he bought ours.

We popped open the champagne our first night there.

Not fully understanding what we'd gotten ourselves into.

We moved into the house in March and planned a party for July, clearing up the acreage for a festive outdoor shindig. It would be a combined housewarming and wedding reception, the one we never had. Family and friends came from afar to join us in the celebration. I prepared elegant dishes we served at Frög. Salmon pâté piped into gladiola blossoms was the hit of the day. The champagne flowed outside, while lines of coke were snorted in bedrooms upstairs.

I had arrived

A destination I'd endlessly sought.

A husband and a home.

The only thing missing was a baby.

We spent a weekend on the beach in Misquamicut, camping out the back of Rickey's Cherokee, the car bought to go with the house. We sat on sand chairs facing the ocean, bottles of beer in our hands, discussing the pros and cons of babydom, me pushing hard for parenthood, with the arms of my biological clock ticktocking in the background. Pregnancy was finally given the green light, this time planned, as we clicked our beer bottles, chugging the contents as fast as we could.

In the meantime, I'd gotten another job. My frustration with the inconsistent paychecks of Lincoln Hall nudged me out of the restaurant business. I accepted a position as a sales rep for a company out of Bryn Mawr, Pennsylvania that sold cookware to college students. A job that enabled me to travel more, an avocation I never tired of.

My getting pregnant seemed agreeable to Rickey, which meant daily intimacy, a notion that suited him just fine. But when I dragged him up the stairs on nights he was tired, sex became a chore. He wanted spontaneity, filled with passion and lust, not scheduled by the time on my gestational calendar. Tension between us started building, which only alcohol could alleviate. I was still drinking up to the time we discovered I was pregnant, as our four months of nightly sex paid off.

We were having a baby the following August
which meant I'd need to give up drinking
a sacrifice I would make for our child
a commitment I wasn't able to keep.

In preparation for becoming parents, we got a puppy, a suggestion by parents who had done this trial run, an idea we both agreed would be a good testing ground. We bought a black Lab we named for our house; Benomi was his official name, a pup we'd end up calling Benny. And a fine initiation it was.

The nighttime crying
interrupted sleep
the constant attention
ongoing peeing and pooping
the dependency
all good training for these parents-to-be.

That year, we were invited to a New Year's party in New York, in an uptown suite rented by Ed, now a big time dealer, with lots of money and drugs to toss about. Bottles of Cristal were popped and after the party goers where significantly buzzed, we made our way down to Times Square, to watch the ball drop, where I waltzed around 42nd Street with a man I didn't know, perfectly sober, not a drop did I drink.

We returned to Ed's apartment where the hard-core partying began. Joints were passed around, while grams of coke were laid on tables, where lines were drawn. I quickly retired to a bedroom, as pregnancy zapped my energy, upset that Rickey was deep into the drugs. He stayed up all night, while I slept intermittently, getting up a number of times to see what I was missing, returning to bed feeling gypped of their glee.

In my third or fourth month, because of my age, I had an amniocentesis done. A huge-ass needle, twice the size they used to evacuate my car-crash hematoma, was stuck into my abdomen not once, but twice, extracting fluids to determine the baby's health. The anxiety building up to this procedure was intense. Not being able to eradicate it with alcohol was a major challenge.

But I was committed to my baby.

I would get through it without the help of booze.

When the results came through, Rickey took the call. Although we both decided to keep the baby's sex unknown, he caved in when asked. And even though I'd told him not to tell me, he couldn't make it through the pregnancy without revealing the gender, consistently calling the baby she. He finally broke down in the eighth month and divulged it was a girl.

The same month I started drinking again.

Five months was my limit for staying alcohol free.

In the last months of my pregnancy, we went to Acapulco, a four-day trip I'd earned through the new job I had, with Rickey accompanying me on the excursion. Our days were spent floating around a lagoon-style pool, our nights, partying in the glow of torches and lanterns, kibitzing with my associates. I was late in my pregnancy and didn't think a glass of wine or two would hurt. One of those nights, Rickey got drunk, an intoxicated state I'd only seen once before.

The pressure of impending parenthood weighed on us both.

Dealing with it the way we knew best.

Back at home, we spent many a night discussing names. I liked Margaux, for one of my favorite wines. Rickey preferred Margaret, the name of his favorite aunt, who'd been there for him in his struggling childhood.

We'd taken Lamaze classes to practice our breathing. And then a week before the baby's due date on August 31, I had a sonogram done that disclosed she was breech, her head pressing against my ribs, a bruise I swore I felt for years. My obstetrician suggested a C-section, a procedure we were both against having. All that breathing we'd practiced would go down the tubes. The doctor pushed for it, afraid of the trouble this big baby might cause, so we scheduled the operation on the day she was due.

I knew it was wrong to drink at this time, but what's a few glasses of wine, was always my reasoning. It won't hurt the baby at this point. So I drank away the grief I felt at losing out on a real delivery. On losing out on the labor and the pushing and all that stuff we'd learned. Having a sister who was a Lamaze instructor only made it worse.

I was feeling sorry for myself.

Always a good reason to drink.

chapter twenty-seven

Oh, For Just One Drink

I make an appointment to see a homeopath, a woman who has M.D. attached to her name. Which means my insurance will cover my visits with her. I sit and talk for 90 minutes. She listens closely to the stories I tell, about my abandonment in childhood that caused asthma to hijack my lungs, and endless years of sneezing that drained my life away. As she sits there and listens, I feel her eyes and ears holding my hand.

She gives me a dose of Nux Vomica, in the form of five tiny white pellets made from the seeds of the poison-nut tree. If taken in large doses it would kill me. But I trust this woman, who will heal me in layers, who is tackling first and foremost, the addictive part of me. I'm glad to have this new woman in my life, as things are escalating with my husband and are not heading in the direction I wish they would go.

I meet with him again in therapy, and at the coaxing of my therapist, I give him a bottom line, feeling a bit nauseous as I deliver the limit.

"I need you to stop drinking before we can get back together."

My stomach flips, as the silence weighs heavy between us.

Our therapist gazes at the two of us, sitting beside each other as we fidget on the love seat. A name that seems a misnomer on this particular day.

She rocks and waits.

Then waits some more.

When the silence seems too much for even her to bear, she says, "So what do you think?" My husband's eyes are glued to the floor. Making eye contact is probably the last thing he wants to do. And I hear the one answer I prayed he'd never say.

"I want a divorce!"

I slip into denial, feeling its warmth surround me, as my therapist looks at me, waiting for my response. I don't know what to say, thinking I may have misheard him. Could my ears already be clogged from the tears that start pouring into them? My mind starts racing, like a tiny car on a teeny track, a mini Indy 500 produced in my brain.

What will you do?

How will you live?

Could this really be happening?

Is this some kind of joke?

A myriad of questions speed around the track, my mind zooms, as my heart's about to cleave. A wrinkle forms on my forehead. I can feel the frown taking over, distorting my face. Tears gush, as that warm cloak of denial slips away, crumpling at my feet.

Oh, for just one drink, right here, right now.

A handful of poison nut seeds might be better.

As I leave the office, his final words ring in my ears.

"You'd better get yourself a good lawyer"

setting the stage for what's to come.

I don't know how to tell my daughter. Acting it out is an easier thing to do. I bang cabinets and slam doors and shamefully kick my innocent dog. My fear twists itself into anger, the fury I thought I'd gotten a grip on, spews like a volcano, raging at the world.

When I go back to see my therapist, I can't look her in the eye. I'd much rather ring her neck than give her a peek at my soul. I'm looking to blame someone and it sure feels like she'll be it.

"Did you know this would happen?" launches from my mouth. My rage dissolves into tears, as my words hurl her way. Before my therapist can gather her thoughts, I want to get up and leave, but that child in me abandoned at three, longs to stick her little thumb in my mouth, and curl up on her lap.

The confusion you feel
is a maze you can't find the exit for
an anger that will suspend your relationship with her
at least for a while.

She tries to reassure me that she didn't really know, though my husband had informed her he'd had sessions with someone else. I feel betrayed once again, this time by both of them. Those moments of forgiveness have long since passed. There's a bitterness on my tongue only a glass of brandy could sweeten up.

Instead, I head straight for the chocolate shop. I ogle the truffles encased in glass, a cast of deep brown confections gathered before me. The girl behind the counter acknowledges my presence, as the chocolate machine purrs behind her. That swirling tub of cocoa goodness I'd like to leap into right about now. I point to the big ones, golf ball in size. My eyes stop at ones that contain Grand Marnier, that orange flavored cognac I use in my cakes.

The brandy you drank on nights on the town
you devour this delicacy in three enormous bites
its richness and goodness wasted on you
this overwrought woman headed for divorce
you sit on the pity pot, where you stay for days.
finally getting your ass up and dragging it to a meeting.

Though I haven't actually told her yet, my daughter gets wind of what's going on from my crazed behavior. It comes in the form of tummy aches that grip her so badly she shivers in pain. I spend nights with her leaning over the toilet. The pain shouts that she needs to throw up. Neither of us realize she's taken on my fear, and no matter how hard she tries, she'll never be able to vomit it out.

My husband tries to rush me along, as his need for getting free of me seems the most critical thing in his life. But I can't be rushed. My way of processing things is far different from his. I can no longer dive into a bottle to drown away my sadness. I know in that alcoholic heart of mine, just one bottle would never do.

So I amp up my meetings and my phone calls to friends. I cry to my group and sob with my girlfriends. I talk with my sister nearly everyday, as my loss is her loss too. We're losing a man we both dearly love. There is no changing his mind, and by the way he behaves towards me now, I know it would never work.

I finally tell my daughter, who cries along with me. I apologize for my incessant weeping, as she wraps her arms around me, telling me not to worry.

"Tears help wash away the sadness, Mommy."

Her wisdom a gift through these difficult times
her being more of a mother than you
a deep concern
and her cross to bear right now.

I start spilling words in the shape of poems. My heart lays flat on the paper, my tears staining pages. These poems will become a chapbook, an idea I have no concept of in these grief-stricken moments. The notion of getting something published feels a lifetime away. Nothing like that matters right now, as just the writing of the words is a soothing salve, a bandage for my bleeding heart. Whenever the pain crops up, opening my wounded core, the words pour forth. They line themselves across whatever I can grab, the back of an envelope, a crinkled scrap of paper, a brown lunch bag, forming poems I never thought I could write.

My daughter and I spend time with friends; having dinner at Sue and Toni's becomes a common event. They become our second family, their kids like a little brother and sister to mine. They fill in for siblings she doesn't have and patch up the loneliness that comes with her only child turf.

Another friend, Burle, also on the journey of birthing a new self, feeds my void and emptiness with words from her goddess research. She lifts the part of me that feels like a female failure.

A woman without a man in her life
is a disgrace to the gender
a message received growing up
and one you hope to replace.

She brings a new set of steps to the CoDA meeting we attend, written by Charlotte Davis Kasl, from her book, *Many Roads, One Journey, Moving Beyond the Twelve Steps*. I feel a tad rebellious, as I take a liking to these novel principles. They pertain more to my life than AA's 12. But rebellion is a part of my Catholic-school upbringing, a response to the precepts that always felt wrong. I'm still recovering from the harm they caused. It will take many years to turn things around, but these new steps are helping me to see myself in a new, brighter light.

The shame of who you are
is slowly being shed
the skin of the viper that ruled your life
left behind.

chapter twenty-eight

Baby Makes Three

I woke up early on August 31st ready to have the baby, preparing a nice sturdy breakfast of ham and eggs with grilled tomatoes from our garden. We'd need the energy for the day that lay ahead, and I needed to stay busy before this overwhelming event took place.

After checking into the hospital at 9:00, I went into labor an hour later, initially delighted that I'd get to be part of the club. By the time they wheeled me in for the C-section at 3:30 or so, I was ready for a drink, though miraculously the thought never crossed my mind. Until they started cutting me open. Though I was numb from the waist down from the epidural they'd given me, the tug of the knife bearing down on my belly caused vertigo so bad I thought I'd pass out. And when the doctor yelled, "Hey, watch what you're doing" to the anesthesiologist beside him, an oxygen mask was quickly attached to my face. I felt so sick, I didn't even want to see our baby.

Rickey held her first.

I stayed in the hospital for a week, back in the day insurance companies were more compassionate to women's needs, but was glad to get home and start our new life together. Little did I know how much this blessed event would forever change things.

Except for my drinking
it would take a few more years

before surrendering to that.

I drank from the day I got home, always around dinnertime, a respectable hour to start. It was widely thought that beer helped produce breast milk, and I was committed to the ritual, both breast-feeding and beer, wanting my daughter to be healthy and strong, never considering I may be passing the alcohol, plus my addiction, on to her.

I was still in denial

which stood in the shadows

waiting for my final bottom to come.

Our life with this baby was not an easy one, as her night time feedings came every two hours, and the resulting brain fog grew stronger each day. Our other baby, Benny, was making it all the more difficult with his daily acts of jealousy, emptying the kitchen garbage and tossing it around.

My mom came to visit and helped with chores. Having a C-section made things difficult for me to do. She cooked dinner for us with a glass of wine always at her side, refilled before it was even empty. A ritual I learned years ago from watching her prepare meals. We connected over this baby, our fights for now were a thing of the past. She took care of me and the baby, something she loved to do, both of us clinking our wine glasses, a familiar and ever-present link.

The first six weeks of nursing were incredibly painful, and the lanolin cream I'd bought wasn't helping at all. I remember one of our first road trips with baby in tow, to a craft's fair in Old Deerfield, on a warm September day. My nipples were so sore, I considered bagging breastfeeding altogether, when it occurred to me to open the window and air them out.

Problem solved.

And nothing a few beers wouldn't assuage.

Company streamed in and out of the house, all coming to see the little one. Corks sprung from endless bottles of wine, caps flipped from bottles of beer, to quench the thirsty onlookers. We were thrilled to show-off our newborn, always glad to have an acceptable reason to down some more.

I went back to work when she was six-months or so, having evenings out, while Rickey cared for our daughter. I was so tired driving home, all I pictured was a glass of wine waiting for me, my baby secondary to that first sip of Beaujolais. My nights became a blur of feedings, praying she'd sleep a little longer after each turn on the breasts, hoping we'd find something that could provide peace for us all.

I remember the night we let her cry, the two of us so tense in the bedroom next door, listening side-by-side while she wailed away. We could only bear a half hour or so, before crying ourselves, our unmet needs connecting too much. I finally got up, white flag waving, and surrendered to her sobs. Through the cold winter months, I nursed her in the bathroom, where we'd placed her cradle and changing table upon bringing her home. It was the coziest room in this voluminous house, needing two wood-packed stoves cranked up high to keep us warm.

Her crying was a rationalization for another beer or glass of wine. Never thinking that those beverages, in fact, might be what's upsetting her little nervous system or causing a colicky disposition every evening through her first six months. Not the onions, broccoli, or cabbage I'd given up in hopes of some respite from her incessant crying, from the pain in her tummy causing her to howl. If it ever crossed my mind that it might be the alcohol I ingested, my denial would eradicate it lickety-split. We rocked her, walked with her, drove her around in the car.

But the thought of alcohol being the cause

was far too much to let in

at a time I felt the need for it most.

When she wasn't crying, we bathed our daughter in the bidet, one of the features that sold us on the house, reminding us of our trip to France, and our pre-baby time together. One weekend, a friend from the company I worked for came to visit. High on pot and wine, we spent time with the baby in the bathroom, blowing bubbles as she sat entranced, howling with laughter as we broke bubbles floating over her head, releasing the stress of responsibility for this tiny person we produced. The first day we brought her home, Rickey declared he felt like a newly elected president, a burden laying heavy on his shoulders. A stress we discharged through our daily consumption and the runs we squeezed into our new parenting lives.

Sometime that winter, on a cold and frigid night, while I was putting on one of my presentations at UMass, Rickey let Benny out to quickly do his business, planning to take him for his nightly walk when I got home. When I came through the door, I knew something was wrong. Rickey's face was streaked with tears, his ease at going to this place something I loved about him.

"It's Benny," is all he had to say. He'd been hit by a car just yards from our house, his black coat making him impossible to see. The two of us cried for a week. You'd swear we'd lost a family member. In fact we had. He was our first baby, who we'd cared for like a child. The one named for the house we lived in. This old relic of a place that fed our need for status, that brought us a feeling of success.

Though it never made up for the loss of Benny, we got a kitty a few months later. She was a gray-and-white kitten from the farm down the road who we called Nellie, the first word our daughter would say. Nellie, whom would be with us through thick and thin and made me sneeze my head off if she was in the house too long, gave comfort to us by her simple presence.

That spring, we had an outdoor fireplace built, as we'd been cooking hamburgers on a makeshift grill I constructed for our reception the year before. We collected field stones from the acreage behind the house. Our land was filled with these New England relics, making turning the soil a huge choir for your garden-variety farmer like me. It would take two weeks, and many wheelbarrows full, to collect enough for the new grill. Which, in the end, became a respite for the fights that would tumble into our marriage not long after Maggie turned a year old.

Before her first birthday, we made a trip to Long Island to see Aunt Minnie and Uncle Frank. The cousins had planned a surprise shower for me, slightly delayed, but most appreciated. It was the weekend my cousin, Steve, reached a ranking he carried for a long time, as he got so wasted at these gatherings, he'd come on to any female who was there, and try to make out with them. This time it was way more than the girls could handle, and talk of forbidding his presence at family parties ratcheted to a new level. It would take Steve another 20 years to get sober. Even being thrown off a redirected airplane because of his drinking, didn't make him stop. Spending a few days in repeat-DUI-jail finally woke him up.

It was at this party I got a call from my brother, John, informing me that our dad had died. My father had climbed into bed on Saturday night, following a quick nine holes of golf. A visit to the clubhouse bar was always essential to the game. My youngest brother, Phil, was snoring down the hall from him, after spending the evening in a local tavern. At some point that night, my dad had called out in fright, evidently knowing his heart was under attack. My brother still recalls hearing his cry, pleading his last words. Thinking it was just a bad dream, my brother stayed in bed and found my father's body the next day.

My sister was away at the time, out west on a rafting trip with her husband and kids, and it was my job to track her down. I found her in Bozeman, Montana, and beckoned her home for the funeral. The family gathered the following week at a memorial service swiftly thrown together by my mother and brother, John. We convened at the lake house, the site of my father's death, the place he loved most, and then headed for the white chapel on the north shore of the lake. There my brother delivered a eulogy, scribbled through tears the night before. It did little to embody the love I had for my dad, or ease my pain, but I was in no shape to furnish a suitable homage.

The apres-memorial party was not a somber one, as alcohol abuse runs circles around my family, contributing in some way to my father's death. I have memories of my mother demanding that I stop crying, as if grieving a parent's passing was a capital offense. "Will you cry this much when I die?" she howled. At that moment, I wasn't really sure. Years of repressed grief sluice forth at times like these. Yet I don't recall her shedding a tear. Her life with my dad overflowed with regrets. And to top it off, my mother had no inkling of the status of my father's ashes and didn't seem to care. Since there was no wake, a decision made quickly by my mother and brother, and not knowing where his body was cremated, I never knew what happened to his remains.

I spent the next few months buried in my garden or inside a glass of wine. The death of a parent is earth shattering, especially the first to go. I wasn't prepared for the unyielding impact it had on my life. Gardening helped; working through pain by kneading soil, I counteracted my powerlessness by crushing grubs with bare fingers. I turned a lovely piece of land that year.

But the thing that helped most
with that outpouring of grief
came in a bottle

my best friend in times of need
always reliable, always there.

The following month, we threw a party for Maggie for her first birthday. A small get-together that Rickey's sister and kids came down from Maine for, plus Maggie's little friends across the way, the twins born just four months before her birth. The good stemware came out, and we celebrated this one-year-old with toasts, never imagining a party without having something to drink. We continued drinking through the night, after our young party-goers left, our tolerance for alcohol had grown, taking larger amounts to get the buzz we always sought.

Through all this, there was a tension building between us, a hole in our marriage that needed to be addressed. I was now attached to my daughter, getting my need for physical intimacy fulfilled through nursing her. My desire for sex had considerably diminished. A red flag I'd brush aside for as long as I could.

Besides, I still had my drinking
always there for consolation
whenever the going got rocky.
But it was seeking to catch up to me
tugging on my sleeve.
a tugging I'd ignore for
a few more well worn years.

chapter twenty-nine

FAS and Food Stamps

My husband is buying another house. Moving on quickly is a thing he does well. He takes our daughter house-hunting with him. He gives her the power you'd only give a spouse. Her place in our lives is a burden she must bear. He moves into a cottage not far from his job, a new home for my daughter, miles away from mine.

He keeps pressuring me to move things along, his need for this divorce far greater than mine. Which leads me to believe another woman is already in the picture. I don't have to poke around too much to find out. The next time my daughter goes down to his house, she's there, having dinner with them. I long to stay calm as my daughter reveals this to me. My head nods as she speaks, while a clawed hand reaches into my chest, grabbing hold of my heart, squeezing it with all its ever-loving might. The idea of him moving on so quickly is a concept I can't begin to grasp, a notion that makes me weep.

The healing power of tears
is still something you're learning about
and trying as hard as you can to accept.

I discover she has children, after asking my daughter too many questions, as honest answers she always supplies. My need to know these things is a danger to my serenity, as my mind ticks away with this new information. I picture my daughter with the brothers and sisters I didn't provide, all of them dining together at my husband's new place, which sends me to my room in a fit of sobs. The only comfort I find is the mourning dove that coos at dawn.

As hard as I try, I can't undo this new-girlfriend-family-vision I've drummed up. My yearning for a drink emerges at night, as I dream of tumblers filled with wine and booze, lined up like soldiers, ready to charge. I toss and turn, trying hard to shake the images. Of course, I stay sober. I know that bar lurking in the shadows is a place I no longer care to go.

My life as a single parent has become much more real, as visions of reconciliation have essentially been erased. It's-all-on-me is an overwhelming idea, and even though I've been doing it for two years, that feeling of back-up has had the floor dropped below its feet.

When alone in the car
you have images of veering off the road
into a thicket of shrubs and trees
a thought while zipping past the orchard
where Kennedy's plane came down.
You don't envision a fatal crash
just enough to land you in a hospital
where a team of loving nurses bring meals
caring for your every wish and whim.

The new course I'm taking presents additional challenges. I need to write a paper as a final project, something I've been lousy at my entire school career. Since alcohol abuse is so near to my heart, I write a paper on Fetal Alcohol Syndrome. I base much of my research on *The Broken Cord*, a bestselling memoir by Michael Dorris. One of the first men to adopt children as a single parent, his three Native American adoptees have the syndrome, and I write about the difficulties they faced. Sadly, he would end his own life in the wake of child abuse charges issued by his adopted children.

My admiration diminishes when I find this out.

The guilt I feel for drinking during my pregnancy becomes my main focus now. Those first few months I didn't know, and the last two months I didn't care, loom large in my head. I start looking at my daughter in a whole new way. Examining is a more precise term to use. Her eyes seem to grow wider apart as I write the paper, her head and upper lip shrink in size. I imagine the things she says sound weird, her thinking grows a bit askew. I flip from side to side in my sleep at night, picturing these aberrations I caused. And beat myself up with these not-so-preposterous imaginary allegations.

I'm also having trouble getting out of bed in the morning. My arms and legs have weights attached to them. I force myself up to wake my daughter, whose bedroom is right next to mine. I fix her breakfast and shoo her out to catch the bus. I watch through windows as she stands alone out there shivering, her body not armed with the fat she needs to stay warm.

The old thermostat that reads 64 degrees
is not enough heat to warm her up
for her 10-minute wait.

I crawl back into bed after she leaves, the grayness in my days too thick to see through. The color in the world seems to have disappeared. My arm is too heavy to pick up a pen and my muse appears to have taken some unrequested time off. My inner critic is clocked in on overtime, and yammers away as I drag through the day. Her nonstop voice is the sole company I keep. My nights are filled with terror, as my husband has pulled back on paying some bills. The sweat in my morning sheets is a reminder of the frights I have while trying to sleep.

I continue to find relief at meetings, my recovery community is still a big source of support. When someone speaks about food stamps, a bell inside me rings, and I know what I need to do next. I make an appointment at the office in Holyoke, not far from the noon meeting I go to there. I wait in a line I never thought I'd wait in and take an interview that buries me in shame.

When my coupons turn up in the mail, it takes days before the nerve arrives to use them. Waiting on line in the grocery store causes my hands to clam up. My eyes shift back and forth in search of people I know. I pray that someone from town doesn't see me here. As I hand over the food stamps to the checkout clerk, my hands shake wildly. My eyes are glued to the conveyer belt. She couldn't care less about what I pay her with, but that information can't be found in my shame-filled brain. I'm certain she'll judge me the rest of the day. Though I'm grateful for this government support, I have trouble meeting other people's gazes. This new batch of slime I'm carting around weighs heavy on the lids of my eyes.

My husband's animosity towards me adds to my indignity. It's reflected in sitting on support checks as he acts out his rage. Those times of willingly handing them over to me are a thing of the past. I now have to ask for them every month. Our days of therapy together are over, so there's no one to hold him accountable anymore. I call one day before dropping off our daughter, the one who benefits from the checks he avoids to send. I remind him to please have it ready, leaving a message on his machine.

When I arrive, he reeks of alcohol and belligerence, threatening to withhold more money than he already has. My frustration boils over, saying I'll tell our daughter about his greed. He rips the check up in my face as I turn and stomp out the door. I drive around till my fire cools down. I return and withstand another round of harassment, until I burst into tears, instantly turning him into this gratuitous other-person. He writes out a check for the full amount.

You are not allowed to be an adult with him
owning your power is a no-no
the sickness in your relationship
is finally sinking in.

chapter thirty

Stumbling Around

A few months after Maggie's first birthday, we got another puppy. Rickey found a Chocolate Lab litter advertised in the paper, its owner located near Dartmouth, not far from where my sister and brother-in-law lived. We picked him up right around my birthday, my present that year, a beauty of a dog we called Rusty. The ache in my heart after losing my dad and Benny would heal a little quicker with this new puppy in my life.

Of course, that grief was also managed with the aid of alcohol.

My brother, Phil, the hardcore drinker in our family, who wandered through life looking for his next high, came for a weekend with his girlfriend, and similar to my history with men, she was one of many he'd have in his rocky existence. My big memory of the weekend was my brother bouncing a balloon off the top of Maggie's head, her giggling, him bouncing, his eyes glazed over from some downers he'd taken, as he guzzled his beers and ballooned her head. He's the brother I'd lost touch with, as his life became too off-the-wall for even me to deal with. While I sought to tone down my use of chemicals, his would increase, taking him places I no longer cared to go.

But I still drank. It was the way I solved my problems. Have an issue that needs fixing? The answer could always be found in a few bottles of beer or a couple glasses of wine. The beverages I switched to in order to hide my dependence from myself.

Though we had a couple of babysitters we could rely on, we brought Maggie with us to most places we'd go. Our trips to Sylvester's for Saturday morning breakfast became a ritual, as did our visits to local pubs. Our child rarely came in the way of the lifestyle we most enjoyed.

We took trips to upstate New York to visit Rickey's brother and sister-in-law, who had a son a year older than Maggie. Though they drank as much as we did, I was often uncomfortable in their presence, as these three educators, all with advanced degrees, possessed a commonality that made me feel left out. His sister-in-law, who had dated my husband before marrying his brother, was a woman of firm opinions who intimidated me. My views seemed wishy-washy and lame next to hers. Her way of delivering ideas were more polished and convincing than mine. She was good friends with Rickey's first wife and frequently spoke of their friendship. I consumed more alcohol when I was with them, cutting the intimidation factor nearly in half, helping to blot out the envy and resentment I frequently felt in their company.

Alcohol has a way of smoothing the edges of self-doubt supplying a confidence that isn't normally there.

My own sister and brother-in-law, whom I felt far more comfortable with, frequently stopped by with their boys on their way home from Panama. They stayed with us for a night or two, to help lessen the load of travel. My brother-in-law was chock full of interesting stories of his transits through the canal, and my nephews always had exciting news about some tropical snake or insect they'd caught or trapped somewhere close to the jungle.

After the kids had gone to bed, we stayed up drinking, swapping tales of our lives. We asked for advice about how to care for a child approaching toddler-hood, as some referred to as the terrible twos, though I could never imagine our daughter in that devilish phase. They invited us to Panama again, as they did most times we saw them. Although the next trip taken there was on my own, a side-excursion I squeezed in on another trip to Mexico with my company. I'd also win a trip to Puerto Rico and two to Hawaii, though my days with that company dwindled as our daughter continued to grow.

At this stage, I was still nursing Maggie, and as time went on and physical intimacy with my husband continued to diminish, the strain between us grew. I had lost my sex drive after having the baby, which had yet to return. Unfortunately, Rickey hadn't lost his. It seemed to increase. I'd gotten to the point that I dreaded going to bed. It felt like another job, one I'd lost interest in doing. So he sought sex elsewhere. With someone he'd hire to do the work.

I found out the weekend my boss and her family came down for a visit. We all had plenty to drink and the guilt of this transaction had obviously gotten too heavy for him to hold. And pathetically, after his confession was over, I stood there holding the guilt, like it was my fault he'd made this decision.

I mean, isn't that what masturbation's for?

I think even the nuns would have approved in this case.

Somehow we got past this, and I tried to oblige as much as I could. But my heart was never into lovemaking after that. He got busier with his work at school, vying for chair of the department he'd worked hard for.

I'd also grown disgruntled with my job—five years of dealing with college students was more than I cared to do. And after making a Sachertorte for a family party, Rickey suggested I start a baking business. One I could do at home while caring for Maggie.

We devised a sketchy business plan over multiple bottles of wine, listing the cakes we thought would appeal to most customers. The über rich Chocolate Mousse Cake with Grand Marnier Crème Anglaise led the band of luscious confections. We found a restaurant-size reach-in on someone's front lawn that we bought and squeezed into the workshop, and bought all the pans and utensils I'd need for these delectable creations.

My mom chipped in for a KitchenAid mixer, the machine at the center of this baking endeavor. Her support meant a lot at the time. After researching purveyors where I could buy discounted ingredients, I asked my friend, Atea, to design a business card, one she produced with elegant script proclaiming Gateaux, Etc. across the top, the name I called my venture. Centered below it, appearing prim and proper atop its pedestal, sat a decadent cake, with icing dribbling down its sides.

I was all set.

All I needed to do was acquire some business.

I spent weeks making sample cakes and delivering them to restaurants I believed could sell my high-end products, ones I learned to bake when I worked at Frög. I followed up with calls requesting responses, "Are you ready to provide your customers with my tasty treats?" Soon orders started coming in and my business took off. I became overwhelmed by it all, and found myself drinking more at night. Always the solution for stressful situations, the only way I knew how to push through difficult things.

But something was different.

I began to notice how much I drank.

It all started with a visit from Ed, who of course, had introduced me to Rickey many years back. He came for a weekend with his kids and seemed like he was doing quite well. After years of abusing his body with alcohol and drugs, he'd gotten sober and was drug free. He went on and on about his new abstemious life, about the meetings he attended, and how good he felt about himself for taking this step. We both squirmed as he yapped about it, gulping our wine and wondering when he'd shut up.

The three of us gossiped about the rest of the family, as we always did, with Ed pointing out who were alkies and the few who weren't. Rickey and I were positioned neatly in the alcoholic ranks, along with the rest of my family and his. After making those disparaging assertions, Rickey and Ed argued the weekend away, fighting over the status of our addictions, neither of them winning in the end.

Alcohol has a way of firming up denial
convincing the alcoholic, they're problem free.

But after Ed left, I couldn't stop thinking about what he said, rolling his words over in my head, feeling them stumble around, wondering if what I'd known in my heart of hearts was actually true. Am I really the alcoholic Ed said I was? When I brought it up to Rickey, he just scoffed at the notion, waved his hand in disgust, saying Ed was on his usual high-horse, assuring me I had nothing to worry about. "After all, you only drink wine and beer. And those tiny bottles of Miller light, at that. What harm can they possibly do?"

After his visit, Rickey's phone calls to Ed dwindled to almost nothing. Staying friends with a recovering person is threatening to serious drinkers, so we kept our distance as much as we could. But I knew deep inside that

Ed was right. I was certain he was right about my parents and his dad, about Aunt Lu and Uncle Bill, about all the kids they passed it down to, except for maybe a few.

I'd store this in a closet of my brain
and take it out a few years down the road.

chapter thirty-one

Strappy Heels

Poems pour out of me. The grief I'm feeling splatters itself across the page.
Since I'm already working in schools, I think it's a good idea to teach kids to
do the same. I create a workshop called *Poems Have Feelings Too!* and apply
for a local cultural council grant to support the work. I even make the local
newspaper, as one of Maggie's teachers, who loves the idea, calls them to come
into the class while I'm running a workshop there.

This helps take my mind off my need to find a lawyer, as pressure from my
husband keeps barreling through. His desire to dissolve our marriage quickly
is a constant source of pain. As tensions mount, my daughter's tummy aches
increase. I look for a therapist for her, one she can call her own, one who will
help her sort through the mess of our lives right now.

She helps her make a chart, to keep track of when her stomach hurts. It feels
more like a homework assignment than something that'll relieve her pain. But
we do it anyway, so when we go back to see the therapist, my daughter has
something to show her, something that makes us both feel accomplished.

The trouble with her tummy lies in your own terror
that thing you're so full of, it's oozing out your pores.

I'm in my last year of grad school, and I can't believe I'm still doing well.
Going at my own pace helps to curb the fear and allows me to get the grades

that feed my confidence, squelching a smidgen of my enormous self-doubt. The doubt I can no longer drink away. I hope to do the same with this divorce. Taking baby steps to the finish line, I hope to avoid the shame of being a divorced woman, a notion drilled into me at an early Catholic age.

Losing the dream of happy-ever-after
may seem closer to the truth.

But I start asking around anyway. I talk at meetings about this impending doom and request advice on who I might call when the time feels right. I hear about a female lawyer who, according to local lore, is a sharkish kind of attorney. It takes weeks before I dig up the nerve to make an appointment. I want to do research on what to ask, though getting books from the library is an equal source of shame.

It matters little this divorce was not your decision.
You are the bearer of its guilt and all its disgrace.

The guilt follows me around like a rabid dog, foaming at the mouth each time I look at my daughter. It's ready to attack as she wrenches in pain, as she leans over the toilet while her slim body shivers and shakes. The powerlessness I feel explodes in my eyes. I want to hold her tummy, like my mom used to do for me, but she doesn't like to be touched in the throes of this anguish. She shakes her head, pushing me away. Instead I get a blanket to drape around her shoulders and a pillow for myself. The tiredness I feel from all this changing, all this letting go, all this helplessness as I watch my little girl, exhausts me to no end.

I go and see this lawyer, who doesn't look at all like the shark pictured in my mind. I tell her my story about getting sober and my husband who didn't care to come along with me. She smiles and says, "It doesn't surprise me. I can't tell you how many divorces I've done with the same set of circumstances, where one person gets sober and the other doesn't." I feel a grin creep across my face, as she has just validated my truth. One my husband would deny if he were sitting here with me. It's a truth that shreds my insides apart.

You thought you were doing the right thing
getting sober, trying to save your relationship
being the mom your mother could never be.
But here you are, sitting in this lawyer's office
discussing steps that will end your marriage for good.

After running through the business side of divorce, I ask how much she charges. My jaw drops at the quote she gives and I say I'll need to think it over. I know full well this lawyer is far out of my range. I drive away feeling a sense of relief, another first I can check off my list. And I think the next lawyer I see, my palms won't sweat quite as much.

My daughter comes home with news of a break-up. My husband and his lady friend with kids have parted ways. I can't help but notice the sliver of hope that penetrates my dreams. This snippet of gossip prancing through the night leads me to think that maybe, just maybe, he's had a change of heart. When I drop my daughter off, I go into the house and try to make small talk, seeing that old glimmer in his Irish blue eyes.

And then there's the gymnastic event, the one held at Northampton High, where our daughter performs with the rest of the acro group I signed her up for. My husband asks me to save a seat for him, which I do with that smidgen of hope still nestled in my chest. The two of us burst with pride as we watch the love of our lives do cartwheels and back turnovers like a pro. We gaze at each other like we used to, before my sobriety ripped it all away.

You leave high on hopefulness
envisioning what might happen inside your head
wondering if he's feeling the same as you.

I dance around for days, playing music that I used to enjoy with him. Ella Fitzgerald singing Cole Porter was one of our favorites. I feel all the romance the music evokes and let myself stay in that place until I take my daughter down to his house a few weeks later. I go in to say hi, but he's left a note that he's out for a run. And then I see them, as I pass his bedroom on my way to the lav.

Laying there
resting on their sides like they fully belong
a pair of high-heeled shoes
strappy and full of sass
ready to light up a cigarette
after a full night of sex.

I say good-bye to my daughter, tears filling my eyes, hugging her tight as her sweaty dad strolls into the house. My hope pops like a balloon that's inflated too much, exploding in my face as I bolt to my car.

Your need for a drink
stabs you repeatedly in the chest
the angst you feel
screams
at the top of its lungs.

chapter thirty-two

Red Flags

We found out my cousin, Liz, the youngest of Aunt Lu's kids, was running in the New York City Marathon and made plans to go down for the race. Tying Rusty out back, we asked a neighbor to check on him, that we'd be home in time to bring him in for the night. We loaded the car with Maggie's paraphernalia and headed to the Big Apple. Lining the race route with Maggie in her stroller, we cheered the racers on with a band of cousins and friends. Lana, Ed, Kathy, Vinnie, Steve, and pals of Liz's from high school and work. Liz finished the race in decent time and we all headed to a restaurant/bar to celebrate her accomplishment. We met Liz's new beau, who would eventually become her husband, and partied with them until it was time to take Maggie back to Lana's to get some sleep.

We continued our celebrating, and decided we were too tired and wasted to make the trip home, totally forgetting we'd left Rusty outside, until Rickey woke at 3am with a start. We quickly packed up our stuff, nearly folding up Maggie's port-a-crib with her inside. We hustled out of there to make it home by dawn, to a young dog howling at the top of his canine lungs, an empty food and water dish by his side. I'd be patching up the holes he dug in my herb garden for days. In the grand scheme of things, it was not the end of the world.

Just another red flag
on the alcoholic shelf in my brain

continuing to frantically wave at me.

By this time, my baking business had taken off to such a degree, I was shuttling twenty or more cakes a week to various restaurants in the area. My days in the kitchen became more frenzied, constantly chasing Maggie out, yelling in high pitches at my baby girl who'd wandered in at bad times. Always finishing off the day with way more than I'd planned to drink. The strain of what I knew about myself was getting harder to hold, so I set a new rule.

I would only drink five days a week.

Tuesdays and Thursdays were off limits.

I wouldn't touch the stuff on those days.

With the exception of holidays, of course.

Maggie was in preschool now, just two half-days a week, which freed me up to get more work done for my business. Around this time, I started noticing an anxiety about being with her I hadn't felt before. I resisted engaging with her when she'd ask me to play a game. Or when she begged for a story like the ones her dad told, after reading favorite books before going to sleep.

My jaw clenched up and my hands grew clammy

anxiety soaring so high, it blocked my ability to make one up.

I couldn't wait to get away from her

causing tremendous guilt

pushing me downstairs for another glass of wine

running from all the causes that ailed me

always drinking more than I should

as my denial continued to keep that knowledge at bay.

Speaking of running, I squeezed in runs at least five days a week, as running was a way to stave off the demons that lurked inside my head. Sweating was always a great cure for hangovers.

We entered races together, the Bridge of Flowers in Shelburne Falls was one of our favorites, a race I'd win in my age bracket the following year. Only two other women ran in the category with me, as I just managed to cross the finish line.

We worked hard at staying functional, keeping the dreadful truth at bay, never wanting to give up that link that held us together.

The link that tied us to family and friends.

The link that was eroding our marriage.

It was in early spring the following year that plans were made for Rickey's brother, his wife, and son to come down from Syracuse for a weekend visit. I went all out with food preparations, spending more than we could afford on high-end items, buying special wines to compliment each meal. I planned gourmet appetizers and desserts, and baked a decadent carrot cake just for the occasion. And then we got the call, the night before they were due to arrive. They couldn't come, for no particular reason, it just wasn't going to work for them. We were crushed, especially me, for all the work I'd put into making a special weekend for Rickey's family. It was a huge let down for us both.

So to heck with the Thursday rule.

It got flung right out the window.

The next day, we made plans to assuage the wash out. We'd take Maggie to the Boston Zoo. But a late start and a stop along the way, got us there five minutes past closing time. Our tolerance for disappointment was wearing thin. And the only solution we knew to deal with it, was to submerge the distress in spirits.

We stopped at a restaurant on the drive back home, parking our car out front in a line of others. We ordered drinks before dinner and a bottle of wine to go with it, then drinks for dessert, hoping to squelch the angst. Both of us were pretty tipsy when we left the place, our daughter the only sober one in the trio. Stumbling to the car, I buckled Maggie into her car seat, looking forward to heading home. But before we'd do that, Rickey banged into the car behind us, cursing about why they'd parked so close, instead of leaving a note or checking for damage. He took off fast, as blaming words shot from his mouth, while we tore down the Mass Pike speeding towards home.

I couldn't believe he'd done this. Already slipping from the pedestal I'd placed him on, this night he had totally jumped off. A life-time of disappointments were flooding over us, and I couldn't stop barking about this particular one. By the time we got home, Rickey had had it. He took off and didn't return until the following evening.

My fear of abandonment went wild

tossing and turning alongside of me
the night he was gone.
I would never look at my husband in the same way.
A sadness lurked in the shadows
waiting for its turn to be heard.

Needless to say, this did not bode well for our already deteriorating sex life. The link between emotional intimacy and physical is a strong one, and we had neither after this event. But my fear of abandonment was so deep-seated, so entrenched, I worked hard at smoothing things over, though my resentment played itself out in our bedroom, an area of our relationship most important to him.

Passive-aggression took over our marriage. Snide remarks were tossed here and there. The more that were flung, the worse they got. The worse they got, the more we drank, forcing down anger with alcohol was the way we both had learned to get through things.

As our life went on and our daughter grew, our marriage continued its walk on thin ice. Rickey had started a new book project, the first textbook he'd ever written, and was excited and frightened by the scope of the venture.

We spent a few days leading to New Year's Eve at my sister's home in Vermont with a group of family and friends. Whenever we were there, my job was to help my sister, a prep-cook to her sous-chef. On the night of the celebration, Rickey asked me to go out with him for a drink before the party began. I was in the middle of making tortellinis with the new pasta maker he'd given me for Christmas.

He kept insisting, telling me if I didn't go, I'd be sorry. He ended up going by himself, telling me later he'd cried in the car. I had let him down immensely, and he would end up sticking to his threat.

As it turned out, I would be sorry.

A punch-in-the-gut kind of sorry.

A sorry that had no way of reversing itself.

chapter thirty-three

All Too Much

I t's my weekend without my daughter, and I've made plans with a friend to meet in Northampton on Saturday night. I park my car and walk to the spot where we'll grab a bite to eat. There's a couple strolling in front of me, holding hands and leaning into each other, chatting away. My heart gasps when I realize it's my husband, canoodling with the sassy-strapped-high-heeled woman, hands held the way he used to hold mine.

You quickly slow your pace
thinking you may throw up
your head starts to spin
as passing out becomes a possibility.

When I meet my friend, I hug her tighter than usual, thinking I may never let her go. I spill my grief all over her newly pressed clothes. It's bad enough I saw them together, but the thought of my daughter spending time with a babysitter for this, makes me want to scream at the top of my lungs. I can't stop kvetching about it, and commandeering the conversation is a thing I don't like to do.

But your pain bubbles over
its only escape is through your lips.

I try hard not to grill my daughter, but I can't help myself. The questions just fly out of their cages, with wings flapping so hard, she almost needs to duck. She's younger than him, by 18 years, not a surprise for a man in the grips of mid-life crisis. She works at the college where he teaches, has never been married, and has no children of her own. I stop her before she can tell me anymore. Chasing those winged creatures back into their cages, I promise myself I won't let them out again anytime soon.

I'm finishing up my last semester of grad school, as graduation draws near. I'll invite my family, as my heart continues to break a bit more everyday. Granted, I've chosen not to be in a relationship, as the only thing I want to be is a good mother to my daughter. But my heart keeps grumbling. Why did he have to bring her to Northampton, the town the two of us once cherished together? I tell myself to snap out of it, to stop this victimization crap, but I can't help myself.

It all seems out of my control.

My family comes for graduation, some of them at least, my mom, sister, brother-in-law, and nephew. I feel grateful and supported by their presence. My sister snaps a picture of me with my daughter and her dad, the awkwardness of this photo shoot smeared blatantly across my husband's face. I am happy on this day, a rare feeling for me right now. I've reached a milestone I never expected to attain, the first in my family to get a master's degree. My accomplishment gleams as bright as the sun on this almost cloudless day. The only cloud comes in a searing remark by my husband about getting the divorce. The threat behind it is palpable, making me want to dig in my heels even more.

Fear is the trigger of control
both of you wrapped tightly in its grip.

And then the unimaginable happens. My friend Sue's six-year-old son, Nicky, has a seizure lasting six hours. When he finally pulls out of it, he has enough brain damage to put him into a vegetative state. Our lives with this adoptive family takes a drastic turn. We are ensconced in a new form of grief, one that reminds me of my childhood, knowing no matter how hard I try, this is something I can't fix. The powerlessness I feel engulfs my life. The thought of doing a divorce right now is the last thing I want to deal with. I appeal to my husband's basic humanity. He backs off, as my daughter and I retreat into more grief.

I multiply my meetings, going more than I usually do, and consider going back into therapy. This event has whisked the carpet from under my already tenuous stance, leaving me afloat. My friend, Sue, is no longer a support, as her life has changed forever.

One night, alone in her room, my daughter scrawls in a notebook of hers. She fills ten pages with *Nicky don't die*, expressing her fear of losing her friend. The sadness from this event has ripped out our hearts and torn them to shreds. I'm on the phone with Sue multiple times a day, her life which tilted sideways before this, has now been turned upside-down and flipped over again and again. I dig deep into an emotional reservoir I didn't know I had, listening as she pours her pain into the phone.

My ears become a vessel for her misery.

Much of my time is spent thinking about this family, who have meant so much to us since my husband left, since meeting this dynamo woman at my CoDA group. I can't begin to imagine what she's going through until my daughter and I visit them, and see the little bouncy boy that Nicky once was confined to a bed, all movement and speech completely gone. His only means of communicating is blinking his eyes.

You leave their house stunned
not knowing how to articulate what you feel
both of you cry on the way home.

Then two months later, another tragedy occurs. The father of my daughter's best friend, who was perched in his hunting stand high in a tree by our neighbor's pond, falls and hits his head on a fieldstone, and dies. Another family close to us has their world torn apart. I feel my heart bleeding as I watch them wade through their cargo of grief.

The thought of going through a divorce
makes you want to drink
you take one look at your daughter
and know you won't.

My husband's patience has begun to wear thin. I find out one day while driving my daughter home from school. He's gotten engaged to the woman with strappy heels. I listen as my daughter talks about the engagement ring I never received, the one the new woman now wears.

You hold in your feelings
until reaching the stairs
to the second floor of your home
racing to your room
plunging onto your bed
soaking your pillow in grief.

I have no choice but to move forward when a sheriff shows up in my driveway. I'm out raking leaves when he opens his door. My body tenses up as he steps from the cruiser. He says my name in a firm and formal way, and I grip the rake as I respond.

He is here to serve you divorce papers
you feel your heart dropping from your chest
shattering into pieces too small to collect
small enough to fit through the tines of your rake.

My hand shakes as he hands me a pen. He needs a signature to confirm I've received the document. The pages of the summons tremble in my hands.

I spend three sleepless weeks, shedding tears more often than my daughter cares to see, before getting the nerve to call another lawyer. I interview two, neither of whom I connect with, wondering if I'll ever find anyone who'll suit my pathetic emotional self.

I think of my neighbor, who brought us cups of Friendly's ice cream a month after she moved in, a gesture that opened my splintered heart. I remember she's in law school, maybe she's the one to ask. I tell her I want a woman who'll be gentle with me. She gives me the name of a classmate, one she highly recommends, alluding to his strong feminine side, saying, "He will handle your case using a pair of kid gloves."

Relief washes over you like a gentle ocean wave.

I make an appointment to see this lawyer and we hit it off right away. I tell him I write children's books, and smiling, he says he does too. He mentions that he represented Eric Carle for a number of years, and I feel my face light up for the first time in weeks, knowing immediately that this is the man I want to hire. After a somber pause he says, "Taking on a client is like a marriage. You must be fanatically devoted. Until it ends." I leave his office with a skip in my step and a tremble in my heart.

You are heading down a road you never thought you'd take
with ruts so deep you fear falling in
swearing your sobriety got you in this fix
longing for a shot and a beer to help undo it all.

chapter thirty-four

March Madness

Maggie was four now and in preschool three days a week. My anxiety about being with her still followed me around, its roots or reasons unbeknownst to me. She was in love with a boy named Bradley, a cute little brown-eyed kid who never spoke to her. She came home and talked about him incessantly, and I'd cringe at the thought of the genes I'd passed along, rolling my eyes inside my head as she rattled on.

Rickey was becoming more and more busy. His schedule filled up with late nights at school, coming home for dinner less a priority than it used to be, reeling off reasons for why he was late. So when my sister called to see if I'd like to go to the St. Patrick's parade with them and my mom, the thought of getting away was enticing, and another St. Paddy's Day party sealed the deal.

Diehard drinkers always look for reasons to imbibe
whether celebrating something or mourning a loss
we'll always find another cause
and St. Paddy's in New York
surely wins the prize.

When they picked me up at noon, I discovered my brothers would be joining us too. Our whole rowdy family, minus our dad, would celebrate the patron saint of all that's Guinness, in the city that never sleeps. Where we could drink as much as we wanted and fit right into the lively crowd. We spent little time at the parade itself (you've seen one, you've seen 'em all), as our thirst for merrymaking directed us into Irish pubs, where music flowed right along with the beer. By 9pm or so, we switched to Irish coffee that would keep us going most of the night.

After drinking way more than we could handle, knowing the drive to New England was out of the question, we headed to New Jersey, to my sister's cottage on Culver's Lake. Starved at 2am, we pit-stopped in Orange for sacks of White Castle sliders, the junk food we were raised on, never ceasing to provide comfort when the road gets rutty. My brothers and I were rowdy and loud, more like a bunch of college kids returning from a frat party stumbling in for these onion-laden belly bombs, than siblings in their 30s and 40s with their mother in tow. We were trashed, yearning to party the night away, and still had to make the drive north to Sussex County.

We drove through West Orange, past both our childhood homes, reminiscing of times we had at these relics of youth, when our dad was still alive, and how much we missed him. We stayed up most of the night, sleeping only a few hours before waking with menacing hangovers and parting ways, our last St. Paddy's celebration where the whole family got smashed.

I was exhausted and worried about going home, knowing what I was facing, a marriage that was falling apart, with no idea how to fix it. But we were in the midst of March Madness, college basketball season was our favorite time of year. Our love for Big East b-ball was boundless. And this was the year P.J. Carlisimo would take my alma mater, the Seton Hall Pirates, not only to the Final Four, but to the championship game. Even Rickey, who was a die-hard Syracuse fan, was behind my team.

One night in the throes of the NCAAs, we went to Fitzwilly's to watch the games. I had repurposed an old headband, the kind with spring-like antennas and some plastic doohickies at the end of each spring that said happy birthday or something similar. Filled with Big East fanaticism, I crafted a THE sign for one spring and HALL for the other, and brought it to Fitzwilly's. We sat at the bar in our usual spots, with our favorite bartender serving us beers. I'd run into him after getting sober and separated, revealing to him my new plight in life. He was glad for me, and wasn't surprised one of us had finally taken the step to quit.

Positioning the headband as he served me another, the weight of the make-shift signs jiggled from side to side, resembling one of those fans the camera zooms in on for televised games. And as my March Madness excitement grew, Rickey sat beside me just plain mad, scowling, and finally declared, "Take that ridiculous thing off your head!" which I refused to do.

The more he insisted
the more I resisted
until he leaned over
and ripped the band off my head.

I sat there fighting him for it, snatching it out of his hand, hopping off my bar stool and storming away. Heading to the restroom, I repositioned this menacing ornament back on my head, strutting out of the women's room like I owned the place. He growled at me, and shaking his head in disgust, he downed the rest of his beer, declaring he was going home. I had no choice but to go with him; my night of celebrating my team was thrown to the floor and stomped on. In an act of utter defiance, I wore the headband home. Neither of us were speaking to one another, the silence louder than any shouts or scream-ing could ever be.

We slept in separate rooms that night
which would soon become the norm.

That summer, we threw a party for our daughter's 5th birthday, a barbecue in the back yard, inviting neighbors, and all her little friends from preschool, including Bradley, the boy she'd crushed on for two years. I went all out, made a beautiful cheesecake decorated with mandarin orange flowers, a cake they hardly ate. We hung a piñata, filled with sweets, from one of our beautiful cherry trees that the kids could thwack away at.

A projection of how we felt at the time.

I was out there, putting on an act, making sure no one knew of the turmoil inside our marriage, or even worse, the turmoil inside my head.

Dress right
make a nice cake
hang a piñata
you'll fool them all.

But I was the one who could not be fooled. I knew something was grossly wrong with my marriage and grossly wrong with me, holding on tight to denial so I wouldn't have to deal with what was catching up to me.

A shoe was about to drop
with the other one
quickly following.

chapter thirty-five

Life on Life's Terms

The heat's been turned up, but I refuse to rush this process because my husband decides to get engaged. Besides, I can't move any faster than I can. I need to gather information so I know what I'm doing, damping down the fears holding hostage of my life.

But most of all, I need to stay sober.

I confer with more women at my CoDA meeting, the one Sue and Burle hardly come to anymore, missing their presence so much it hurts. These other women provide different strategies for me to take. Some advise me to go for the house, others suggest I take part of his pension. They all agree to get as much as I can for that precious daughter of mine and myself. The notion seems greedy and makes me feel queasy, as confusion sprints circles in my head.

I need help to sort things out, and decide to seek more counseling. On a visit to my daughter's therapist, I ask if she can also see me. I need therapy more than my daughter does now. She reluctantly agrees, and so do I.

She's not the kind who hugs when you need it
or looks at you with compassionate eyes
or jots down every little thing you say.
she's not the kind you'd ever choose
bottom line, she's not Renée.

But I need a professional to talk to, who will help me climb through the car wreck of divorce. So I make an appointment, and apologize to my daughter for stealing her shrink, as desperation has once again taken over my life.

Each month now, I'm forced to ask my husband for the support check, as he resents more than ever having to give me one. His new honey-bun has no children. I sense her understanding of child support is limited, due to his resentful remarks. When my daughter goes down there on weekends, it's often to stay with a babysitter. Her dad's attention is on this fiancée of his, who seems to care less about my daughter than the pricey wines and dinners at fancy restaurants my husband provides.

The ones he used to bestow on you
back in the days you drank like her.

The jealousy I feel makes me loathe myself. Though it doesn't stop me from grilling my daughter when she returns from his house. I need to know all that goes on when she's down there, producing cabinet slamming and cuticle picking, plus far more junk-fooding than I'd like to admit. I've padded on pounds since he demanded the divorce. I wear bulky clothes to hide the extra weight from myself and others. I don't feel as much pain when I'm stuffing my face, and quickly realize I may be replacing the booze with food.

You wish it didn't matter but it does
the constant chatter in your brain
from all those concealed messages
yammer away
telling you so.

I hobble through my days with my head hung down. The thought of making eye contact is unsettling to me. Getting divorced leaves a scarlet letter upon my furrowed forehead. I spend far too much time saying I'm sorry to my daughter, attempting to alleviate the guilt this failed marriage produces. I sense any apologizing will only come from me.

I get calls from Sue nearly every day, and hold her grief as best I can, failing miserably to compare my angst with hers, which I just can't help but do. My victim-self is in high gear now, a divorce I never wanted being forced on me.

But after listening to her heartache concerning her precious son, my victim-hood disintegrates. It dissolves into a culvert of feelings, swirling itself away.

I write like a maniac, pouring grief into verse, discernible relief with each word that's put on the page. Though the poems aren't any good, I try not to care. The fact I'm even writing amazes me still, and is a welcome outlet during this precarious and grief-filled time. I now have a master's degree, this so-called portal to a better life. I sadly lack the sense of self I need to make other major life decisions, though the urgency assaults me each night I crawl into bed.

Soon, the holiday season descends on us. My desire to evade it is something I just can't do. So I take my daughter and dog to the tree farm down the road, suppressing the sadness this ritual evokes. My daughter will be with her dad this year, and my sister and brother-in-law in New Jersey with my mom (a trip too much for me to take right now), so I'm spending the holiday alone.

We hunt down a Balsam, our favorite kind of tree, as Rusty runs through the rows sniffing the best ones out. After finding a beauty, the softer back-and-forth kind, we saw it down and haul it home in my daughter's red wagon. It's a Hallmark card in the making, though a depressing one at that. I hide the hurt that lurks inside, waiting until my daughter's in bed, spilling buckets of pain onto my tear-stained pillow. The loss of my marriage along with the other sorrows of this year soak my pillowcase. I wish the season would slither away.

Since housecleaning has become a thing of the past, the boxes of decorations linger in the hallway for months on end. Laundry baskets overflow onto dusty floors and stacks of unopened mail teeters atop the washer and clothes dryer. My brain is too cluttered with the reams of divorce advice I read and receive. I can't deal with anything else. My lawyer gives me numerous options. The magnitude of these decisions loom so large, I have visions of running away, something I dream of doing at least once a week. But now the tug's so strong, locking myself in the house seems the only safe thing to do. The amount of self-pity I feel is way beyond what is needed, doing little to move things along. After all, this is what I signed up for when I got sober, living life on life's terms.

But as you hunker down
atop that pity pot of yours
you can't help but think

a good stiff drink
would feel really good
right about now.

chapter thirty-six

Lowest of Lows

Maggie started kindergarten while our marriage crumbled around her. I continued baking cakes, each day becoming more and more aware of some impending doom. Rickey would leave the house early, hardly saying good-bye, and I'd drag myself out of bed to get Maggie ready and on the bus for school. After she left, all I could do was crawl up the stairs and climb back under the covers. The heaviness I felt pulled me down into a dark gloomy place, until she arrived home at noon, came upstairs, and poked me awake. I spent the rest of those days in a daze, baking and delivering cakes, with Maggie in tow, and then trudged through preparing dinner for a man who seldom came home.

I had broken my days-of-the-week drinking rule by then, now casting aside Tuesday, the only abstemious day left, which made me drink that much more. I held tightly to my wine and beer guideline and drinking before 5:00, which kept my denial deftly in place, though that inner-self shoulder-tapping was getting harder to ignore.

One weekend, after ongoing evenings of eating alone with Maggie, I finally confronted Rickey. I remember we were sitting on our bed, unusual for that time in our life, and I took his hand in mine, staring into his eyes as I asked the question that had stomped inside my head for months. "Are you seeing someone else?" He tried pulling his hand away, but I held on tight, while sweat collected on his clammy palm. He looked me in the eyes and flatly denied it, as beads of perspiration swarmed above his upper lip, his mouth forming the smirk he gets when his discomfort is more than he can contain.

At that moment

I chose to believe him

this man who in some excessively codependent way

I still loved.

One night, when he came home late and I'd asked him where he'd been, his indifference filled the room with its chill. I became so frustrated by his detachment, I picked up the phone, pulled it from its plug and pitched it across the room at him. It missed, but it was a warning that could no longer be ignored.

Soon after this incident, I started nagging him about seeing a counselor, something I had previously thrown into conversations when things got too heated and obvious that we needed help. He was against therapy, ruffling at the thought, always hostile to the notion of having to divulge our dirty laundry to someone else.

So we went on like this, sleeping in separate rooms, him being detached, me feeling angry and desperate. I bought endless boxes of hair dye, not sure which one I wanted to be, settling on a platinum shade of blonde, a sassy Marilyn Monroe-ish color that would surely catch his eye. In the end, I had to ask him what he thought, his degree of seeing me these days was at the minus stage and the pain that followed brought me down to my lowest of lows.

Drinking was the only thing that would prop me up.

I drank as much as I could, without passing out.

He went away one weekend in October, a stretch of time I spent pining for old boyfriends, scouring frayed address books for phone numbers I hoped they still had. After making us cheesy scrambled eggs for dinner and tucking my daughter into bed, a bottle of cabernet by my side, I dialed Doug's old number, surprised when the voice who answered was his. We talked for nearly an hour, catching up on our lives, my end of the conversation slurring as we rambled along, hanging up feeling a mix of elation and shame for having called him.

I finished the bottle and opened another, drinking away the guilt I felt, along with any remaining glee. I'd polish off the second bottle before crawling into bed. As soon as I closed my eyes, the room started spinning, circling me with all its secrets, screaming *you drunk* as it whirled and twirled, until I could do nothing but lean over the side and puke out my guts. I tried cleaning it up, with a towel I grabbed after stumbling my way to the bathroom, pushing around globs of scrambled eggs mixed with wine, rearranging pieces of the night's shambles.

The next day, when Maggie came into my bedroom, stepping into my mess and asked, "Oh Mommy, are you sick?" I knew the gig was up.

I kept drinking for another two months, doing everything I could to make myself attractive again to this man and this illusion I clung to. The man who had left our marriage almost a year before, who relished our daughter's every move, as he intentionally ignored my existence with each passing day.

He finally agreed to do therapy with me, a woman we'd see in the town where he worked. The fact that she was late for our appointment turned me off considerably, having to sit with Rickey in utter silence felt excruciating. I had trouble hearing anything she said after she finally arrived, rattling on about her tardiness like we'd been friends for years. The only thing that really stuck was her suggestion we do something special, which much to my surprise, we actually followed up on.

We secured an overnight babysitter and made a date for New Year's Eve.

Little did I know, it would be the end of my drinking years

and the beginning of a life

unimagined.

chapter thirty-seven

A New Life Has Broken

The year before our divorce becomes final is filled with sleepless nights and hand wringing. I discover the term decision fatigue, fitting my new life as a single mom. Decisions about my daughter, about my ramshackle house, about this life that's opening up to me.

And always the decision not to drink that day.

I have numerous meetings with my lawyer, whom I've gotten to like. My neighbor was right. He's smart, professional, and gentle with me. I decide on what I want. The house is a priority in hopes of making me and my daughter feel secure. I go back and forth for months between my husband's lawyer and mine, until most of the nit-picky things seem to be smoothed out.

The day arrives for the hearing and I can't decide what to wear. My indecisiveness frequently shows up when I'm picking out clothes. Should I wear the tight purple jeans that sing a free-spirited tune or the denim jumper that reeks of the stability I craved when we first split up? I choose a pullover given to me by my friend, Burle, made of luscious purple chenille that dives at my breasts and a skirt with paintings of camels lumbering through a starlit night, one I bought last year at the Goodwill store.

A fitting frock to end a marriage.

I arrive at court, greeted by a barbed-wire guard who frisks my soul, as the distress I feel oozes from my pores. My lawyer ushers me down the hall, his fast words fill my ears, making me dizzy as he speaks. My gut clenches and churns, knowing I cannot bite into the bones they throw my way. I follow him to a crowded corridor, with lonely people lining benches on either side, like the first immigrants at Ellis Island. I see my daughter's dad sitting amongst this crestfallen group.

He throws me his grin, as tears tumble down my face and hundreds of spectators witness my grief. A woman takes me by the arm, offering me a quiet space. I long to say no, as this anguish I feel craves ceaseless recognition. She sits with me, feeding me tissues, and notices my pin, rattling on about angels. I press a smile to my lips and secretly wish her away. I finally get called into court and my sadness subsides as the judge smirks at my soon-to-be ex, noting his previous appearance before this bench.

You'll be back in two months to finish the process
when you'll finally agree on the details of this dissolution.

When it's all over, I leave the courtroom, and amble towards my car. I pass shop windows garishly attired for Valentine's Day and wonder why I labored over what to wear. Crossing the street, I see his Jeep Cherokee which draws me in and I peek into the back seat, noticing status quo strewn about. Childlike curiosity walks me to the pub where we argued and smooched on Saturday nights. Gazing in the window, I see him sulking, alone, sucking amber lager on the stool that used to be mine. Dryness saturates my throat, as I open the heavy glass door and ride the wave of nausea that carries me over to where he broods.

"Hi Rick," pours from my mouth as he turns and gapes, perplexity tucked into his eyes. Asking me to sit, the nausea resurfaces and I wonder why I'm here. Moving away from the bar, the two of us muddle beneath the arch of a tiny alcove, as a flurry of discomfort fills the air. I ask for a hug, forgetting how it feels, and find it hard to pry myself away.

We crumble over words; what does one say in the throes of divorce? Would he mind picking up our daughter to save me the time? He glances at his watch and winces, so I awkwardly suggest food, and he agrees before knowing what's happened. He plans an escape if an argument ensues, and my practical response surprises us both.

We walk to a favorite Latin grill, serving only soda to extinguish the heat.
Embarrassment smothers his face, as a dollar bill is his only exchange.
And while he runs to a nearby ATM
you sit dipping corn chips
into spicy green salsa
sensing a new life has broken
with your daughter's dad.

Epilogue

My mom lived to be 90, after spending her last four years in a nursing home. Much to her dismay, she was sober the years she was there. My siblings and I were incredibly grateful for having that time with her. None of us could believe she lived that long. I spoke with her on the phone every other day and I was able to heal my relationship with her before she died. I kept a promise that I would not let her die alone and was there, in a cot next to her hospital bed, when she took her last breath. We buried my dad and mom's ashes in the same plot, chuckling about the fact they'd have to spend eternity together.

In 2002, Bull Thistle Press published a chapbook of the poems I wrote about my grief and divorce entitled, *DIVORCE PAPERS*, with the help of Greg Joly, a homesteading editor who corresponded with me by snail mail. And in 2006, my picture book, *WHEN THE COWS GOT LOOSE,* was released by Simon & Schuster, with the sweet and funny Kevin Lewis herding it on to publication.

My daughter is now a therapist at a residential program that treats teenagers with mental illness, trauma, and attachment issues; she remains my pride and joy. Her dad married the woman who wore the strappy high heels I spoke of in these pages, who sadly died in 2006 from effects related to alcohol abuse.

I spoke in tears at her service.

Alcohol kills one person every 10 seconds worldwide.
—World Health Organization

Helpful Resources

The National Council on Alcoholism and Drug Dependence (NCADD) questionnaire might help you decide if you have a problem with alcohol.
*See my score below

Am I Alcoholic Self Test:

1) Do you drink heavily when you are disappointed, under pressure, or had a quarrel with someone? YES NO

2) Can you handle more alcohol now than when you first started to drink? YES NO

3) Have you ever been unable to remember part of the previous evening, even though your friends say you didn't pass out? YES NO

4) When drinking with other people, do you try to have a few extra drinks when others won't know about it? YES NO

5) Do you sometimes feel uncomfortable if alcohol is not available? YES NO

6) Are you more in a hurry to get your first drink of the day than you used to be? YES NO

7) Do you sometimes feel a little guilty about your drinking? YES NO

8) Has a family member or close friend expressed concern or complained about your drinking? YES NO

9) Have you been having more memory "blackouts" recently? YES NO

10) Do you often want to continue drinking after your friends say they've had enough? YES NO

11) Do you usually have a reason for the occasions when you drink heavily?
YES NO

12) When you're sober, do you sometimes regret things you did or said while drinking? YES NO

13) Have you tried switching brands or drinks, or following different plans to control your drinking? YES NO

14) Have you sometimes failed to keep promises you made to yourself about controlling or cutting down on your drinking? YES NO

15) Have you ever had a DWI (driving while intoxicated) or DUI (driving under the influence of alcohol) violation, or any other legal problem related to your drinking? YES NO

16) Do you try to avoid family or close friends while you are drinking?
YES NO

17) Are you having more financial, work, school, and/or family problems as a result of your drinking? YES NO

18) Has your physician ever advised you to cut down on your drinking?
YES NO

19) Do you eat very little or irregularly during the periods when you are drinking? YES NO

20) Do you sometimes have the "shakes" in the morning and find that it helps to have a "little" drink, tranquilizer, or medication of some kind?
YES NO

21) Have you recently noticed that you can't drink as much as you used to? YES NO

22) Do you sometimes stay drunk for several days at a time? YES NO

23) After periods of drinking, do you sometimes see or hear things that aren't there? YES NO

24) Have you ever gone to anyone for help about your drinking? YES NO

25) Do you ever feel depressed or anxious before, during, or after periods of heavy drinking? YES NO

26) Have any of your blood relatives ever had a problem with alcohol? YES NO

Understanding Your Score:

A "no" is scored 0, and a "yes" is scored 1. So the score you get reflects the total number of questions that were answered "yes." A score of 2 or more indicates that you may be at greater risk for alcoholism.

If you answered "yes" to between 2 and 8 questions, you should consider arranging a personal meeting with a professional who has experience in the evaluation of alcohol problems.

If you answered "yes" to more than 8 questions, you may have a serious level of alcohol-related problems requiring immediate attention and possible treatment. You should seek professional guidance.

* I answered yes to 16 of the 26 questions, which indicated a significant cause for concern.

Disclaimer: *The results of this self-test are not intended to constitute a diagnosis of alcoholism and should be used solely as a guide to understanding your alcohol use and the potential health issues involved with it. The information provided here cannot substitute for a full evaluation by a health professional. Test © 1984 updated 2015 NCADD. All rights reserved*

Am I Codependent Self Test:

1. I am in a significant relationship with someone who is addicted to a substance or behavior, someone who is depressed, or someone who is very needy. YES NO

2. I have difficulty saying "no" when people ask me to do something, even when I know I should not do it. YES NO

3. I feel I need to cover up for irresponsible people in my life because I don't like to see them in distress. I'd rather "fill in and help them" than see them suffer consequences. YES NO

4. I believe it is my job to fix, manage, and hold my family and my relationships together. YES NO

5. I work hard to be thoughtful and nice to others and get angry when they fail to appreciate or reciprocate my efforts. YES NO

6. I like to be around people that need my help. I feel lost if I don't have a role or duty to fulfill. YES NO

7. I worry about how I make people feel. This preoccupation strongly affects my own feelings. YES NO

8. I don't like being alone. I need to be around others in order to feel alive. YES NO

9. I am afraid of people. I need to isolate in order to feel safe. YES NO

10. I fear being abandoned or rejected, and I go to great lengths to be liked. YES NO

11. I believe being "good to myself" is equivalent to selfishness. YES NO

12. Other people's needs always take precedence over my own, even if mine are urgent and theirs are not. YES NO

13. If something about my life or myself is less than perfect, I see it as a failure and become defensive if others comment on it. YES NO

14. Deep down inside, I don't really like myself and don't want people to know the "real me." YES NO

15. I tend to blame and criticize people and circumstances for my feelings. YES NO

16. I have a hard time leaving relationships, even if they are unhealthy. YES NO

17. I have a difficult time asking people for help, even when it's necessary. YES NO

18. I find it difficult to speak what I truly feel or ask for what I need. YES NO

19. I like to keep secrets, because I fear that if others knew my problems, my image of being the "strong one" would be ruined. YES NO

20. To avoid feeling guilt and shame, I seldom speak my mind to people who disagree with me. YES NO

21. I tend to see people and situations as "all good" or "all bad." YES NO

22. Though I try to please people, I often feel isolated and alone. YES NO

23. Because I value the opinions of others over my own, I always worry about their opinion of me. YES NO

24. I have difficulty talking to people in authority, as I feel inadequate. YES NO

25. I am confused about who I am or what I want from my life. YES NO

26. My life has become unmanageable as a result of my dysfunctional and unhealthy relationships. YES NO

Understanding your score:

Answering yes to more than five of these questions can indicate your life has become affected as a result of dysfunctional and/or unhealthy relationships. I answered yes to all but one before I started recovery and only two after I worked the steps and spent a number of years in therapy.

Notice: Please note that answering yes to the majority of these questions should not be taken as a final determination in establishing that you have a problem with codependency. This questionnaire is merely a guide to help raise awareness on whether you are affected by this condition. The questions have no clinical backup and should not be relied upon as a substitute for professional diagnosis.

The 12 Steps of AA/CoDA that help guide members towards recovery:

1) We admitted we were powerless over alcohol/others—that our lives had become unmanageable.

2) Came to believe that a Power greater than ourselves could restore us to sanity.

3) Made a decision to turn our will and our lives over to the care of God as we understood Him.

4) Made a searching and fearless moral inventory of ourselves.

5) Admitted to God, to ourselves, and to another human being the exact nature of our wrongs.

6) Were entirely ready to have God remove all these defects of character.

7) Humbly asked Him to remove our shortcomings.

8) Made a list of all persons we had harmed, and became willing to make amends to them all.

9) Made direct amends to such people wherever possible, except when to do so would injure them or others.

10) Continued to take personal inventory and when we were wrong promptly admitted it.

11) Sought through prayer and meditation to improve our conscious contact with God as we understood Him, praying only for knowledge of His will for us and the power to carry that out.

12) Having had a spiritual awakening as the result of these steps, we tried to carry this message to alcoholics and to practice these principles in all our affairs.

Where to find an AA meeting in the US or Canada:
http://www.aa.org/pages/en_US/find-local-aa
Where to find a CoDA meeting: http://locator.coda.org/

16 Steps for Discovery and Empowerment by Charlotte Davis Kasl, Ph.D., from her book, *Many Roads, One Journey: Moving Beyond the 12 Steps* © Charlotte Kasl. Originally published by HarperCollins. These steps helped change my life, and are presented here with permission from Dr. Kasl and HarperCollins.

1) We affirm we have the power to take charge of our lives and stop being dependent on substances or other people for our self-esteem and security. Alternative: We admit/acknowledge we are out of control with/powerless over _____ yet have the power to take charge of our lives and stop being dependent on substances or other people for our self-esteem and security.

2) We come to believe that God/Goddess/Universe/Great Spirit/Higher Power awakens the healing wisdom within us when we open ourselves to the power.

3) We make a decision to become our authentic selves and trust in the healing power of the truth.

4) We examine our beliefs, addictions, and dependent behavior in the context of living in a hierarchical, patriarchal culture.

5) We share with another person and the Universe all those things inside of us for which we feel shame and guilt.

6) We affirm and enjoy our intelligence, strengths, and creativity, remembering not to hide these qualities from ourselves and others.

7) We become willing to let go of shame, guilt, and any behavior that keeps us from loving ourselves and others.

8) We make a list of people we have harmed and people who have harmed us, and take steps to clear out negative energy by making amends and sharing our grievances in a respectful way.

9) We express love and gratitude to others and increasingly appreciate the wonder of life and the blessings we do have.

10) We learn to trust our reality and daily affirm that we see what we see, we know what we know, and we feel what we feel.

11) We promptly admit to mistakes and make amends when appropriate, but we do not say we are sorry for things we have not done and we do not cover up, analyze, or take responsibility for the shortcomings of others.

12) We seek out situations, jobs, and people who affirm our intelligence, perceptions, and self-worth and avoid situations or people who are hurtful, harmful, or demeaning to us.

13) We take steps to heal our physical bodies, organize our lives, reduce stress, and have fun.

14) We seek to find our inward calling, and develop the will and wisdom to follow it.

15) We accept the ups and downs of life as natural events that can be used as lessons for our growth.

16) We grow in awareness that we are sacred beings, interrelated with all living things, and we contribute to restoring peace and balance on the planet.

Books that helped me to recover and heal:

The Language of Letting Go: Daily Meditations for CoDependents
  by Melody Beattie
Many Roads, One Journey: Moving Beyond the 12 Steps
  by Charlotte Kasl, Ph.D.
Healing the Shame That Binds You by John Bradshaw
The Dance of Anger by Harriet Lerner, Ph.D.
Feel the Fear and Do It Anyway by Susan Jeffers
Understanding the High-Functioning Alcoholic by Sarah Allen Benton
The Journey From Abandonment to Healing by Susan Anderson
The Body Keeps the Score by Bessel van der Kolk, M.D.

And these titles by Brené Brown:

Women and Shame
The Gifts of Imperfection
Daring Greatly
The Power of Vulnerability
The Gifts of Imperfect Parenting

Internet communities that specialize in recovery:

The Fix: www.thefix.com
The Temper: www.thetemper.com
Addiction Unscripted: www.addictionunscripted.com
AddictionBlog: www.addictionblog.org
SMART Recovery Blog: www.smartrecovery.org/blog
SheRecovers: www.sherecovers.co
SoberMommies: www.sobermommies.com

Acknowledgements

I'd like to thank the following people who supported me through the process of writing this book, as well as those who are still in my life, even after I wrote about them.

First and foremost, my beloved daughter, Maggie, who pushed me to write a memoir, due to her love of the wild stories I told at family reunions. Neither of us knew when I started, it would become a journey through my alcohol use and recovery. She's been my go-to person, especially during the arduous months of the pandemic, putting up with hundreds of FaceTime calls and my ongoing anxiety. I am supremely grateful for her keen editorial eye, her sympathetic ear, and her loving support.

My next thanks goes to my sister, Sui, and her husband, Phil, who gave me honest feedback on the many contenders for cover design and for their heartfelt approval of the one I chose. My sister, who's always been my biggest cheerleader, has read and offered praise and feedback of many of my early drafts, since my writing days began. I value her opinion greatly; to my brother, John, who not only sings me the Beatles' "Birthday" song every year, but showed genuine interest in my project; and to my younger brother, Phil, for feigning the same.

Of course, I wouldn't be the writer I am today without the love and support of my dear writing group: Linda, my walking buddy, chief grammarian and faithful sounding board, who stayed by my side the whole way; Nancy, for saying it was the best thing I'd ever written after hearing only one chapter; Tom, my veggie partner, who always made me laugh and delivered valuable critique; and Elaine, who I miss.

A huge thank you to my publisher, Naomi Rosenblatt, who took a chance on this memoir and whose kindness and patience with me is beyond measure. And my publicist, Jen Maquire, who jumped in and enthusiastically joined our team.

I am eternally grateful to my therapist, Renée, who held my hand with compassionate eyes as I poured out my heart in our years of sessions, and who read an early draft of the first chapter, giving me the encouragement I needed to continue and a recommendation that I used.

Speaking of early readers, I'd also like to thank Rita, who gave me solid advice on my first chapter. And my high school friend, Janet, who along with her husband, Peter, graciously read some early chapters, and Kim, who tried. And special thanks to all my other OLV friends, who've rallied around me on FB and cheered me on, like the pep rallies we had in high school.

I am thankful to my extended family: Lana, who sent the perfect card that said, "Only You Can Write Your Story the Way It Was Meant to Be Told"; Liz, my baseball pal, who provided some photos and rooted for me from the West Coast; and my dear cousin, Merry, for all our adventures, who I've been friends with since our birth, just one-week-apart.

To my Panama family: Becky, Matt, and Andrew, who along with my sister, have prayed for my success; Elyse, who has no judgement in her pure accepting heart, and her brother Mark, who plans to read my book aloud, at the dinner table, for the whole family to hear.

To my friends: Burle, who helped me become the woman I am now, by introducing me to a feminine deity, and has quelled my anxieties through this often stressful writing and publishing process; Trina, my first sober friend in recovery, who early on, told me my first chapter was far better than the many others she's read and that my memoir would get published soon; Helene, who once sang her version of "Your Song" kneeling before me on my birthday, and who believed in me when I couldn't believe in myself. I just love you, Chil; Sue, who welcomed Maggie and me into her family when we were lost, and taught me ways to heal myself, so I could write; Leslie, who encouraged me to submit my first personal essay to Salon; Stephan, who guided me through my divorce and supported my writing about the journey; and to Jodi and Sue T, who gave me a platform to help kids write poems loaded with painful feelings like mine. I cherish you all.

To all my addiction writing friends, who taught me to be vulnerable and brave; and to my AA and CoDA groups, who not only helped me stay sober, but encouraged me to love myself when I thought it was impossible, and to shed the shame and fear I carried for years.

To all my Binder friends, especially those in the memoir group, who besides helping me navigate this seven-year-process, their hard-earned wisdom ushered me through episodes of crippling self-doubt, picking me up and urging me on. And to Susan Shapiro, who opened a door for me at Heliotrope Books.

To Maggie's dad, Rickey, who helped me bring our pride and joy into the world, and who, after all we've been through, is still in my life. We've come a long way. For that I am grateful.

To my mom and dad, who though they are no longer with us, did the best they could.

To my grand-kitties, Wonton and Wasabi, who always make me laugh and open my heart when they say goodbye from the window.

To all my readers, some who may be struggling with addiction and recovery, or divorce and single parenting, or know someone who might be, I send a big hug. I hope this book helped.

And finally, to those I may have forgotten, please forgive me.

I love you all!

CPSIA information can be obtained
at www.ICGtesting.com
Printed in the USA
BVHW081604290421
606131BV00001B/45